THE MICROCHIP:
Appropriate or Inappropriate Technology?

THE ELLIS HORWOOD SERIES IN
COMPUTERS AND THEIR APPLICATIONS

Series Editor: BRIAN MEEK

Computer Unit, Queen Elizabeth College, University of London

The series aims to provide up-to-date and readable texts on the theory and practice of computing, with particular though not exclusive emphasis on computer applications. Preference is given in planning the series to new or developing areas, or to new approaches in established areas.

The books will usually be at the level of introductory or advanced undergraduate courses. In most cases they will be suitable as course texts, with their use in industrial and commercial fields always kept in mind. Together they will provide a valuable nucleus for a computing science library.

Published and in active publication

THE DARTMOUTH TIME SHARING SYSTEM
G. M. BULL, The Hatfield Polytechnic

THE MICROCHIP: APPROPRIATE OR INAPPROPRIATE TECHNOLOGY?
Dr. A. BURNS, The Computing Laboratory, Bradford University

INTERACTIVE COMPUTER GRAPHICS IN SCIENCE TEACHING
Edited by J. McKENZIE, University College, London, L. ELTON, University of Surrey, R. LEWIS, Chelsea College, London.

INTRODUCTORY ALGOL 68 PROGRAMMING
D. F. BRAILSFORD and A. N. WALKER, University of Nottingham.

GUIDE TO GOOD PROGRAMMING PRACTICE
Edited by B. L. MEEK, Queen Elizabeth College, London and P. HEATH, Plymouth Polytechnic.

DYNAMIC REGRESSION: Theory and Algorithms
L. J. SLATER, Department of Applied Engineering, Cambridge University and H. M. PESARAN, Trinity College, Cambridge.

CLUSTER ANALYSIS ALGORITHMS: For Data Reduction and Classification of Objects
H. SPÄTH, Professor of Mathematics, Oldenburg University.

FOUNDATIONS OF PROGRAMMING WITH PASCAL
LAWRIE MOORE, Birkbeck College, London.

RECURSIVE FUNCTIONS IN COMPUTER SCIENCE
R. PETER, formerly Eotvos Lorand University of Budapest.

SOFTWARE ENGINEERING
K. GEWALD, G. HAAKE and W. PFADLER, Siemens AG, Munich

PROGRAMMING LANGUAGE STANDARDISATION
Edited by B. L. MEEK, Queen Elizabeth College, London and I. D. HILL, Clinical Research Centre, Harrow.

FUNDAMENTALS OF COMPUTER LOGIC
D. HUTCHISON, University of Strathclyde.

SYSTEMS ANALYSIS AND DESIGN FOR COMPUTER APPLICATION
D. MILLINGTON, University of Strathclyde.

ADA: A PROGRAMMER'S CONVERSION COURSE
M. J. STRATFORD-COLLINS, U.S.A.

THE MICROCHIP:
Appropriate or Inappropriate Technology?

ALAN BURNS, B.Sc., D.Phil.
Lecturer in Computer Science
University of Bradford

ELLIS HORWOOD LIMITED
Publishers · Chichester

Halsted Press: a division of
JOHN WILEY & SONS
New York · Chichester · Brisbane · Toronto

First published in 1981 by

ELLIS HORWOOD LIMITED

Market Cross House, Cooper Street, Chichester, West Sussex, PO19 1EB, England

The publisher's colophon is reproduced from James Gillison's drawing of the ancient Market Cross, Chichester.

Distributors:

Australia, New Zealand, South-east Asia:
Jacaranda-Wiley Ltd., Jacaranda Press,
JOHN WILEY & SONS INC.,
G.P.O. Box 859, Brisbane, Queensland 40001, Australia

Canada:
JOHN WILEY & SONS CANADA LIMITED
22 Worcester Road, Rexdale, Ontario, Canada.

Europe, Africa:
JOHN WILEY & SONS LIMITED
Baffins Lane, Chichester, West Sussex, England.

North and South America and the rest of the world:
Halsted Press: a division of
JOHN WILEY & SONS
605 Third Avenue, New York, N.Y. 10016, U.S.A.

© A. Burns/Ellis Horwood Ltd. 1981

British Library Cataloguing in Publication Data
Burns, Alan
　　The microchip. – (Ellis Horwood Series in Computers and their Applications)
　　1. Computers and civilization
　　2. Microcomputers – Social aspects
　　I. Title
　　303.4'83　　QA76.9.C66
Library of Congress Card No. 81–4187　AACR2

ISBN 0–85312–261–X (Ellis Horwood Ltd., Publishers – Library Edn.)
ISBN 0–85312–353–5 (Ellis Horwood Ltd., Publishers – Student Edn.)
ISBN 0–470–27206–6 (Halsted Press)

Typeset in Press Roman by Ellis Horwood Ltd.
Printed in Great Britain by R. J. Acford, Chichester.

Table of Contents

Author's Preface

Over the last few years, computerised equipment has moved away from being merely a specialist tool to one which encroaches upon all members of society. This proliferation of modern technology in the developed nations has been widely publicised and is a result of economic and, in some instances, military influence. It is now time for those who operate this technology and those who are affected by it to exert influence and control over its deployment. This will only be achieved if a mutual understanding is reached between the technician and the consumer in order to determine the criteria by which the effects of such technologies can be assessed.

The aim of this book is to present such criteria, based on the concept of the 'appropriateness' of technical systems and tools. It builds upon the classical works of Illich, Dickson and Schumacher by dealing with microelectronic applications within developed nations rather than concentrating as they have, on third world technology. This is not to ignore the far greater problems of the developing world but reflects the author's belief that the use of appropriate technologies is of crucial importance to all societies. The role of high technology is not yet clearly defined and needs careful consideration. Technologists and scientists must accept responsibility not only for the efficiency of the equipment they devise, but also for the wider socio-economic ramifications of their work.

This book looks at a wide range of microelectronic applications and considers a number of them in greater detail, drawing upon the author's research into designing energy efficient heating systems, community education programmes, and decision support and control systems. It should appeal to students of computer science at college or university, those involved in teaching the subject, people who work with computers and anyone who is interested in the way such technologies interact with the pattern of society. Topics covered include the impact of the microchip upon employment, education, privacy and information handling, as well as the development of appropriate tools in the fields of analysis, control, entertainment, domestic appliances, energy saving technology and alternative social structures.

It would be impossible to thank all those who have directly or indirectly helped me to formulate my ideas and put them together in the form of this book. I must, however, explicitly mention Haleh Afshar, Roger Haines, George Hay, William Hall, Mike Horwood, Chris Jones and Douglas Kell. I am also indebted to Ulla Wyberg for preparing the diagrams. Finally, I must give special thanks to Carol Burns and John Galloway for editing the script, even when the author didn't want them to, and preparing the manuscript. Acknowledgements are also gratefully given to all authors whose work is quoted and, where applicable, their publishers for granting permission to reproduce this material. Such publishers include North-Holland, Fontana, Victor Gollancz, Routledge and Kegan Paul, Sphere Books, NCC, Input Two-Nine, McGraw-Hill, Springer-Verlang, Abacus, Addison-Wesley, MIT, Monthly Review Press, Viking and Universe Books.

Alan Burns
Bradford, March 1981

Glossary of Terms

Access time — time taken to extract an item of data from secondary storage.

Ada — new, very powerful high-level language.

Assembly language — a programming language in which the programmer uses mnemonics which can easily be translated into specific machine language instructions.

BASIC — simple high-level language, used primarily on microcomputers.

Binary digits — Bits — the digits 0 and 1 as used in the binary number system.

Bonding — the fixing of minute connecting wires onto a single integrated circuit (Chip).

Bus — a group of parallel wires that connect together two or more computerised devices.

Ceefax — a computerised information system run by the BBC television authority.

Central Processing Unit — CPU — the control centre of a computer.

Chip — a substrate containing a single integrated circuit.

Circuit board — the base onto which the chips are placed which provides the means of communication between the various items of the system.

COBOL — a high-level language used primarily for commercial applications.

Compiler — a program that converts a high-level language program into an assembly or machine code set of instructions.

Convivial — a term used to depict socially responsible technologies.

Data Base — a structural collection of computerised information and data.

Electronic mail — the transmission of messages between computerised equipment, usually along conventional telephone wires, which bypasses the conventional mail services.

Embedded system — a device or machine whose actions are being determined by a pre-programmed internal computer.

Expert system — a sophisticated program that attempts to 'learn' by interacting with experts, and then uses this knowledge to instruct non-experts in such activities as medical diagnosis.

FORTRAN — well established high-level language, used mainly by scientists.

Hardware – a term used to indicate the physical units which constitute a computer system.

High-level language – a programming language in which statements represent symbolic actions rather than machine code instructions.

IEEE-488 bus – a particular bus used to connect laboratory-type equipment.

Informatics – information technology – the combination of theories concerned with information storage and retrieval, and the technologies required to perform these tasks.

Large scale integrator – LSI – an integrated circuit with over a hundred components.

Machine language – the language that the computer can act on directly.

Mainframes – large computer systems.

Memory – the part of a computer that stores the data and program instructions.

Microchip – a popular term for a single integrated circuit.

Microcomputer – a computer whose CPU is a microprocessor.

Microinstructions – the organised sequence of control signals that cause the computer to obey machine language instructions.

Microprocessor – the CPU of a small computer held on an LSI.

Microsecond – one-millionth of a second.

Millisecond – one-thousandth of a second.

Multiprogrammable – a computer system that can be used by more than one user at a time.

Nanosecond – one-thousand-millionth of a second.

Operating system – a complex set of programs that run on a computer to control its operation and provide a simple environment for the machine's users.

Oracle – a computerised information system run by the IBA.

Parallel processing – the running of two or more programs simultaneously.

Pascal – well structured high-level language, used primarily by computer scientists and some microcomputer users.

Peripherals – the input and output devices attached to the computer.

Prestel – a computerised information system run by BT (British Telecom).

Process control – the automatic controlling of industrial processes by computers.

Programs – a sequence of instructions, ordered to perform a particular task.

Port – the connection by which peripherals are attached to microcomputers.

Random access – where all storage locations in memory can be accessed in the same amount of time.

Secondary storage – an area of memory on specialised peripherals.

Software – a collection of programs whose execution controls the hardware.

Viewdata or Videotex – a general computerised information system which includes the display of data on a TV-type screen.

1

Two Views of the Future

"Western society is experiencing a series of technological revolutions which is changing our society and our economy as profoundly as did the Industrial Revolution." (Stonier 1979b).

It is the opinon of many commentators and social analysts that Britain, together with the rest of the developed world, is on the brink of a major economic and structural upheaval. The whole fabric of society is envisaged as being under threat, and the cause appears to be the application of a minute piece of silicon. The chip, or microchip as it is popularly known, will lay the foundation to a new cultural order which has already been given such names as the post-industrial society, the third industrial revolution, or even the third wave (Toffler 1980). What all such considerations have in common is the belief that microelectronics, because it is such a fundamentally new technology, will profoundly affect all areas of our existence.

To many, the availability of cheap, reliable and extensive processing power, as opposed to the expensive older variety, will have such an unpredictable effect that anticipations of the likely social impact can only be obtained by looking for parallels from the past. Undoubtedly the greatest radical change our society has yet encountered was the initial industrial revolution. In the early 18th century, prior to disruption, 92% of the population worked on the land; with the harnessing of steam for industrial power and improvements in agricultural technology this figure was reduced dramatically. This mass exodus from the farm to the city established today's position where only two or three of every hundred working people are employed in the production of food, yet this is sufficient to keep at least the developed world well fed.

The 'first' industrial revolution represented the extension of man's muscular abilities by the use of external power. By comparison, the second industrial revolution, which was due to the harnessing of electricity and the development of transporation, can be viewed as the use of technology to extend our senses and mobility. The railway network and use of the telephone and radio have affected all our lives just as the movement from agriculture had done before. For the micro to be the instigator of a third industrial revolution it must catalyse similar social reform.

It is easy to isolate the main properties of microtechnology which could bring about such change. Firstly, in manufacturing its application can lead to enormous increases in productivity that would greatly reduce the need for people to work in this sector. Secondly, by improving methods of communication, the service and information industries could expand beyond all recognition to become the dominant element of the economy. Electronics is not essential in an information society but it is a convenient vehicle for represenation; it bears the same relationship to information as steam did to energy — not a unique but, nevertheless, a useful embodiment. Proponents of the new economic order, that is the post-industrial society, visualise a future community in which less than 10% of the workforce are needed in agriculture and manufacture to produce all the food and goods required by the remainder who are employed in information handling. The movement from rural employment to manufacturing in the first industrial revolution is mirrored against our present transition from manufacture to service.

Informative as this analogy might be, it should not be taken too far because it is inaccurate in a number of aspects. The growth of industry and agricultural output was spread over a relatively long time; the present 'revolution' which is due entirely to the sophistication of microelectronic components could occur more rapidly. Moreover, the service industries are not new; they are as old as manufacture itself, and even before the birth of the micro, over 50% of jobs were concerned with information processing. A rise from 50% to perhaps 80% is significant, but hardly a revolution, unless the service side is also subject to considerable restructuring.

Microelectronics opens up a vista of applications which, understandably, have been the subject of much analysis, especially with respect to their wider social implications. Unfortunately this debate has not produced a coherent view of the full effects of the 'new technology'. In essence, two distinct opinions have emerged, namely those that are optimistic and those that are not. The optimist looks to the promised land with the microprocessor finally freeing humankind from the toil of labour and the fear of war, whereas the pessimist sees merely mass unemployment and the depersonalisation of life and work. These two extreme views form a useful starting point from which to examine the application of microelectronics. They illustrate both the extent to which people will prophesise and the very real need of a systematic assessment of microtechnology, if any worthwhile future planning is to be achieved.

1.1 THE OPTIMIST
Continuous Technological Growth — Infinite Social Adaptability
Christopher Evans, in his popular book *The Mighty Micro,* depicts the optimistic view. He believes that there is no end to technological growth and that the

micro will continue at an exponential rate to become cheaper, faster and more powerful. Its application area will expand and, moreover, society will adapt freely to all such innovation and change. Productivity levels will soar, an expansion which will be accepted and welcomed by first the majority of the western and then the global population. No matter how obscure, insignificant or apparently irrelevant a gadget or gimmick, there will still be a ready market to warrant its mass production.

Recent evidence with digital watches, calculators and computerised games does indicate that once the 'market' starts to vigorously support such devices it may well be able to induce near infinite consumption. The optimist and pessimist will agree on one point: the influence of microtechnology will be both extensive and emphatic. Our homes, work, leisure, education, health, communications and social orders will all be open to restructuring thanks to the availability of processor power. The microcomputer is an extension of our intellect and must therefore transform all aspects of our lives. To illustrate this consider the following applications, expected in the distant and not too distant future.

Information Technology
Electronic chips will continue to be made more extensive so that increasingly bulky literature can be stored electronically. When the stage is reached whereby over one hundred thousand words can be stored upon a single chip then books, particularly novels, will become available on minute slices of silicon rather than paper. Traditional printing will become economically unviable; the book of the future will consist of a hand-held set, ergonomically designed to be similar to a good quality book, into which the latest 'micronovel' will be placed. The viewer will display a short section of the work at whatever magnification the reader's eyesight demands. Additional features will include automatically keeping your place at the point at which you closed the screen.

Considerably more information will be available in the home, via advanced viewdata systems at a cost which a domestic budget can afford. Colour displays will be in every room, and within a fraction of a second any data that might be required will appear in either graphic or character form. As the storage capacity of the chip increases, whole libraries will become available for everyone to have at home, in the briefcase or even in one's top pocket. Books, of the screen type, will become more intelligent by performing such functions as automatically translating the text into whatever language is required; and, when the reader gets tired, they will take over and read aloud, again in whatever language is wanted.

Encyclopaedias, also available on a single chip, will 'do their own research' by bringing together all the information that they have on a topic for which the user wants background knowledge. Information that must be communicated between colleagues, friends or family will be transacted directly between viewdata sets; there will be no need to perform the tedious task of transcribing the data onto paper and then physically moving it to the required destination. In the rare situation where a typed copy is needed, a printer that will accept voice input will replace the present method of hitting keys.

The Individual

The cashless society appears to be an inevitable consequence of the micro revolution. Money, in terms of actual coins and notes in one's pocket, will disappear and in its place everyone will have an 'intelligent' bankers' card upon which a small microelectronic device will be attached. At the time of any sales transaction the card will be placed into what was once a cash till, and the goods purchased will pass in front of a laser powered reader that will recognise the products and calculate the bill. The customer's bank account will then be checked to ensure that sufficient funds are there and, if so, the cost of the purchases will pass directly from this account to that of the retailer. This system is already in operation in small areas of the United States, although it has met with varying reactions; in an economy based upon credit, instant direct debit is far from attractive. Theft of this all-important card will be protected by fingerprint recognition on the card itself.

Other gadgets that will become indispensable to the modern man about town will include a watch that memorises telephone numbers and addresses, calculators that talk, and two-way wrist communicators that will enable one to be in constant contact with the office. Car transport will also witness changes to include a range of useful devices: head and sidelights will come on automatically when night approaches, the fuel gauge will be given a voice to make it more noticeable, and personalised ignition will prevent theft. The fuel mix and engine tuning will become micro controlled for greater efficiency, and radar type equipment will help stop accidents. Routes will be planned for the driver that will take account of up-to-date traffic information coming from the local Carfax[†] station. Communications facilities will be available in all cars, but in tomorrow's society there will be far fewer reasons to drive anywhere. Video conferences that can link together any number of people will become the normal means of 'meeting' colleagues because of their efficiency in terms of speed and the increasing cost of transport in the post-industrial, oil-scarce society.

The Home

It is perhaps in the home that the greatest changes will take place. The 'home computer' will become as essential a piece of domestic equipment as the washing machine or cooker, and just as a house is now wired for electricity and piped for water it will, in the future, be 'wired' for information. Communication channels, presumably using fibre optics, will run through the entire building and be available in every room.

[†]Carfax is a system already in operation that interrupts radio programmes to give local traffic news.

No element of traditional home life will be spared the helping hand of the micro; Davis and McCormack (1979) in their book *The Information Age,* depict the following optimistic view of the family domicile:

"Houses will contain sensors built into walls, roofs, furnaces and pipes. These sensors will, in turn, be hooked in to the home's computers. Any leak, any potential problem in wiring or heating will be instantly relayed to the home's computer that will, in turn, notify you of the need for repairs or maintenance. The automatic fire alarm will sound at almost the instant smoke is detected, and the automatic phone hook-up will simultaneously notify police and fire departments.

The home computer system will probably be used to turn lights, appliances, and entertainment equipment on and off at set times. Your computer, for example, can control your tv cassette recorder, allowing you to watch 'The Tonight Show' at eight in the morning. Do you like coffee when you first get up? The computer will turn on the coffee pot, wake you up, and run your bathwater. If you enjoy games, your home computer will provide a partner for chess, a dealer for blackjack, or a wheel for roulette.

Burglaries probably will plague society in the future, as they do now, but your home computer system will be connected to sensors placed in windowsills, doors, and other likely points where an intruder could enter your home. Even if the burglar alarm system were disarmed, it is possible to set up a fail-safe second line of defense. Equipment exists to create an electronic field and to sense any disturbance of that field. By simply moving in the house, the burglar would trigger the alarm. Your system will sound a signal, dial the police, turn on the lights, and play a recorded tape of vicious-sounding Doberman Pinscher barks and growls.

This same system might be set to turn on your oven, defrost your refrigerator, and water your plants. It might remind you, too, of maintenance tasks only you can perform, such as changing your storm windows or raking leaves."

Interestingly, most, if not all, the gadgets mentioned above are available now and have been for a number of years. Some homes in the USA are already heavily computerised, and systems such as central heating or cooking which can be activated via the telephone, from outside, are on sale now in the UK (how you prevent someone ringing up the with the same equipment and turning the cooker on four hours early, is not yet clear!). The optimist's home will be a completely controlled but personalised environment where every need (well, almost) will be anticipated and fulfilled in a totally relaxed atmosphere which is just as well as considerable amount of time will be spent there.

Work

"Once computers infiltrate a society, their virtues override any intrinsic objections to their use, and their continued infiltration and ultimate domination is from that point inevitable. They achieve their subtle take-over by demonstrating first their usefulness and, when that has been established, their indispensability. The laws of survival in the modern world apply and those companies that employ computers to their maximum effectiveness will achieve a monumental economic advantage. Those that reject or ignore them will sooner or later find themselves in ruins". (Evans 1979a).

That computers will take over work is irrefutable, and this must be to our eventual benefit even though, at first, large-scale redundancies, short-time working and early retirement will bring a host of social problems. Boring work, by definition, is repetitive, and repetitive work is just what robots are good at; therefore the unattractive jobs in our society will become the forte of the machine. Similarly, dangerous work will become increasingly unacceptable, and automated systems in the mines and chemical plants will become the norm.

No area or work will remain unaffected by the micro; manufacture will be undertaken by robots, and data handling by automated information systems; even the professions will eventually be superseded by intelligent machines that will organise education, diagnose illness, and adjudicate in legal disputes. Whether this means the end of work as we know it or just a radical restructuring with other jobs being created to replace the redundant ones is still not clear, but obviously the role of work will never be the same again. It will no longer dominate our lives, in terms of hours spent or significance given. Moreover, these changes will come about quickly; we will not have the luxury of indulging in planned social change — it will be here before the end of this decade.

Education and Health

These two pillars of society, which in Britain have formed the basis of our welfare state, will change out of all recognition by the turn of the century. Teaching machines ranging from hand-held dictionaries to complete classroom systems will, to a great extent, replace the human teacher. Schools themselves may decline in importance when the home information system supplements, or even supersedes, traditional methods of education. It is not, however, only the children that will need or require education; all ages in a rapidly changing society will be demanding retraining and refresher courses. This demand will be impossible to satisfy if the potential of automated computer-aided teaching is not fully utilised.

In health care changes will be even more significant. When a patient arrives at the local GP surgery, she or he will not be met by a nurse or a receptionist but by a computer terminal linked to a national data processing network. This computer will contain complete records of the patient, and built into it will be routines for undertaking the preliminary diagnosis. Having done this it will produce a report and recommendations to the doctor who will then decide on the course of treatment. Few GPs can have a working knowledge of the complete range of drugs currently available for prescription; the computer system will have such knowledge and will be able to advise the doctor on the most apposite medication for each patient.

Possible side-effects of drugs can be monitored by the national network; if a new specialised drug is brought into use today, perhaps only one or two patients per doctor would be prescribed it. This sample is too small for all but the most obvious and consistent side-effects to be noticed. With an overall medical monitor, determental effects could quickly be highlighted and the drug taken out of use. When everything else is equal the cheapest form of the tablet or medicine would be recommended, and with computerised dispensing equipment the exact quantity of drug could be given. These two facts alone would probably pay for a national computer in only two or three years.

Doctors and surgeons of the future will be trained by computers that have learnt from previous experts in the field. This ability of intelligent machines to learn from interacting with humans may even be put to good use in psychoanalysis:

> "Current experiments with computer-interviewing . . . suggest that patients can strike up a surprising rapport with the computer, particularly in sensitive areas such as those involving psychosexual or emotional problems. Might not the very much more powerful machine intelligence of the late 1990s, trained to respond to every nuance of a patient's voice, patterns of speech, hesitancies, even his (sic) facial expressions and eye movement, provide exceptional relief and perhaps, therapy?". (Evans 1979a)

One area in which the micro is already providing considerable help is in the development of aids for the handicapped. The automated home will be a boon to people who have limited mobility, and 'intelligent' wheelchairs with many robotic features will have a similar role outside. In addition, individuals who suffer from visual and hearing disabilities will find an increasing number of electronic aids on the market, particularly voice controlled equipment. Some injuries, such as a severed nerve, may even be bypassed by some appropriate microelectronic appliance.

In the long term the micro may well find more of a role in preventive medicine. External apparatus will continually monitor the somatic functions and broadcast alarm at any irregular or inadvisable behaviour. Internal probes equipped to sense malignant cells may be implanted in patients at risk so that the earliest warning of possible cancer growth can be given. There is really no limit to the number of uses that the micro can be put to in health care.

The Government
International organisations and governments will become more dependent on computers to fulfil their administrative and political objectives. Economic planning will be almost entirely taken over by sophisticated computer controlled models which will finally make economics an exact science. Democratic control will be maintained by 'instant elections' and referenda in which the people are asked, via their viewdata communication network, to give their opinions on whatever is the subject of the moment.

As computers become more intelligent — the generic term for future computers is UIM, Ultra Intelligent Machines — they will systematically gain control over functions and roles currently considered exclusively human. For instance, Professor J. McCarthy of the Artificial Intelligence Laboratory at Stanford

University has remarked. "What do judges possess that we cannot tell a computer?". A UIM would contain detailed knowledge of the defendant's previous convictions, if any, and would have access to a vast store of case history upon which to base its decision. New laws would be instantly accommodated and might even be initiated by a UIM suggestion. The important thing to remember is that judgements would be correct!

A considerable amount has been written about the possibilities, and in some cases realities, of computer crime. The primitive systems of today are open to this type of abuse, especially as such crime is only a relatively recent one and the police, as yet, have insufficient expertise to deal with it. Tomorrow's systems will be far more secure; most computers will be accessible only to those personnel the machine actually recognises as having clearance; finger print checks or even skin resistance tests will prohibit unlawful entry to the system. As a further aid to crime fighting, personal identifiers based upon a single communication chip will enable the police to check the whereabouts of all citizens at all times.

The basis of this optimistic view is that if change is inevitable, as appears to be the case, then there is no reason why it should not be for the better. As people in an information society gain more knowledge they will have greater control over their own lives and more freedom from the state. But to get the most from this technical revolution, attitudes must change and quickly; society must be sufficiently adaptable so that this image of a golden future will be realised. In particular, the wealth created through the widespread use of efficient microelectronic based machinery and services must pass to the population at large, who will then buy the goods and use the services necessary to sustain the economy. A truly brave new world is ahead.

1.2 THE PESSIMIST
Continuous Technological Growth – Zero Social Adaptability
The pessimistic view is based upon a resignation to the inevitability of a continuing exponential growth in the electronics industry, and a fear that the social changes needed to meet the resulting cultural upheavals will not happen at anywhere near the rate necessary. Technology growth will continue because the primary users and the technology manufactures have a vested interest in it doing so; the remaining population have no say in how the machinery should be controlled and gains little direct benefit from its deployment. There is no structure in any western nor eastern, economy which guarantees that the advantages obtained from this technology will rest with ordinary people, for as Braverman points out:

> "The remarkable development of machinery becomes, for most of the working population, the source not of freedom but enslavement, and not of broadening the horizons of labour but of the confinement of the worker within a blind round of servile duties." (Braverman 1974).

Two issues which provoke great concern, and form the foundation of the pessimistic outlook, are the future of work and the fear of the Big Brother State.

Work
> "The people who develop and control technology are not interested in the quality
> of our lives: they are only interested in increasing profits. So instead of building
> a new world of freedom and leisure, new technology is bringing the fear of mass
> unemployment to the hearts of millions." (CIS Report 1980)

Work forms an essential part of our lives but, unfortunately, the cost of labour has consistently increased over past centuries, so that in many industrial processes it forms the major expense. Tools and systems that can reduce this labour cost will therefore be universally welcomed by manufacturers.

All the elements of production will be affected by the micro; in the developmental stage computer-aided design equipment will reduce the number of personnel in the drawing office and planning department. Even more serious than this, though, are the consequence of microtechnology for the shop floor. Numerically controlled machine tools are replacing conventional equipment in all areas of industry. Though the computing components of these tools are becoming progressively more sophisticated, their costs are falling steadily; today they constitute perhaps 10% of the overall price as against the 40% of fifteen years ago. A CNC (Computer Numerical Control) machine tool still requires an operator but it is doing work of maybe eight machines, leaving their operators redundant. Following the CNC equipment onto the shop floor comes the robot and the automated assembly line.

From car manufacture to chocolate packing, the most labour intensive element of production is the assembly of the final product, and that is therefore where most effort will be focused in the introduction of new systems. Manufacturers find themselves caught in a Catch 22 position; to employ the same number of workers they must retain their share of the market by remaining competitive, but if other firms are increasing their efficiency by the use of new technology, then the only way to remain competitive is to make similar rationalisations by laying off staff. Companies are forced to either cut their labour costs or go out of business altogether.

Though factory workers are quite familiar with the pressing demand for greater productivity and have accommodated new skills in order to achieve it, office personnel have been working in an industry that has changed very little over the past fifty years. This situation will not continue, for electronic equipment is already revolutionising the office. Copy typing will disappear, filing will be done automatically as will data processing, and all communications will be carried out by electronic mail. A vastly diminished flow of business letters will lead to refinements in the telephone system resulting in increased reliability and automation. The impact of this upon employment will be devasting; clerical work (traditionally female) will virtually vanish and the Post Office, being the largest employer in Britain, must suffer considerably from this 'progress'. Another alarming aspect of the communications revolution is that office work can easily be transferred around the world. This will lead not only to manufacturing taking place in the third world, for cheaper labour, but also data processing and document preparation. This would exacerbate unemployment in the developed world whilst being of little real benefit to the emergent nations.

The net result of all these effects will be gross and permanent unemployment on a scale as yet unknown. It may be that in the long term attitudes to work will alter, but the protestant work ethic is deeply rooted in our society and will not be removed overnight. In the interim we face the prospect of having many millions of 'second class citizens' who may not be happy just to sit back and accept this role.

Big Brother is Watching!

Unemployment, however bad, is not a new phenomenon in our society, even if in the future it will be of unparalleled severity. By comparison, the use of sophisticated electronics to monitor an individual's every move is a new and sinister development which will have far greater effect on our way of life in the so-called post-industrial society.

In the future it will be possible for security forces to record each person's movements, wherever they may be, by making it compulsory for everyone to wear a communication beacon. This development would be considered by most people as an infringement of civil liberties, and it is unlikely that this situation could actually arise in a democratic society. There are, however, examples of company systems that come close to these ideas. Computerised factories are currently in operation where all personnel must carry an identification card to gain access to each area of the factory through electronic locks. This card does not just unlock the door, it also records the event, therefore a worker's progress around the buildings can be followed, and such activities as clocking on and off are done automatically at the main gate.

Computerised cash registers are becoming a familiar feature of the modern supermarket; they work efficiently and have a number of special functions not available on the standard till. One of these enables the operations of the person working the register to be timed. In Denmark's largest supermarket chain, strong union pressure forced the employers to remove this adjunct. This was after a total refusal to work with the registers following a chance discovery that the employers were, in fact, monitoring every action of the machines. New technology word-processors are also capable of automatically measuring the work efficiency of typists in a manner not known or understood by the typists themselves.

The office and supermarket are only two examples of what could be a general application of microprocessor equipped tools. If one's job has anything to do with a microcomputer then it is possible, and in many instances likely, that your ability to work with the machine will be continually recorded for your employer. It is rare for any job to consist entirely of interacting with a computer, therefore to take just one measurement as an evaluation of overall performance and, moreover, to do so without the knowledge of the employee is a gross misuse of an employer's power.

In an information society all data, including personal records, is kept in computerised data bases. These computers will be linked together to form networks and give the effect of there being just one enormous file containing information on every member of society. This file will be open to local and national government officials, tax officers, the police and security forces. Additionally, unlawful and unsanctioned access to the file will make a mockery of any concept of privacy in tomorrow's society, for no matter how modern the equipment, there are always means of 'getting into' the data bases, especially if you have the backing of expertise and equipment.

The pessimistic consequences of computerising personal information are highlighted by the following questions: Is it reasonable for your employer to have access to your medical and possible criminal records? Should a credit firm be able to check all your bank accounts? Is it right for tax inspectors to automatically have knowledge of every financial transaction you make? Would you be happy for commercial organisations to know that you have not bought a television for five years nor taken a holiday abroad for three, and to be sent unsolicited advertising because of that knowledge? Should the police know where you spend your money, how much you have and how much you earn? Should government officers have access to all your personal records?

There is at least one more disquieting feature of this technology that should be related; the libraries of the future will not be collections of printed books but visual display units where all reading material can be obtained, from a novel to a government report. It is not unheard of for books to be banned and the mere possession of sensitive material to be an offence. Even with technology currently available it would be possible to restrict access to material and monitor the reading habits of the nation. In the name of national security, will such data be used to draw political conclusions about individuals? Freedom of information has a somewhat hollow ring to it when its consequences are fully appreciated.

The Ownership of Technology

The electronics business is one of the world's fastest growing industries, and this will presumably continue to the end of this century and beyond. IBM, the gigantic computer manufacturer, can amass over $5 billion[†] gross profit per year and spend $1 billion of that on research and development. The rewards from this area may be high, but so too is the cost of taking part. Small firms cannot compete in the production of 'new technology', and the faster this technology changes the more likely it is that manufacture will be concentrated in just a few large multinationals, based either in the USA or Japan.

[†] 5 thousand million

Tomorrow's society will depend heavily upon electronic equipment. If its production is under the control of only a few companies then they will have immense power. Simon Nora (1978) has warned the French government of the possibility of IBM becoming 'one of the great world regulatory agencies', and the democratic authorities in the USA have already witnessed the difficulties inherent in trying to restrict IBM. In 1977, Indonesia attempted to nationalise the distribution and servicing of foreign goods; IBM's response was to threaten total withdrawal from the country, which would have left the government's computer systems inoperative. The Indonesian authorities backed down, being too dependent on the technology to consider any alternative strategy (source: *Asian Wall Street Journal*).

If a government cannot control the use and distribution of computer technology and microelectronics, what chance does an individual have? Information technology will rationalise most aspects of everyday life and make it virtually impossible for anyone to contemplate any alternative lifestyle. In a cashless society you must have a direct-debit card and an 'open' bank account or you will not even be able to use the local shop. If all information comes from a VDU linked to a central system then failure to have this equipment will prohibit one's access to books, magazines, newspapers and government data; it may even eliminate one's democratic right to vote in elections. To work, pay taxes, or visit the doctor will necessitate computerised data files being kept on you. There is no choice; if you are a member of society you must play the game, and play it according to the 1984 version of the rules (date chosen at random).

Optimistic or Pessimistic?

Many of the very real fears expressed by the pessimist are of fundamental importance and will be described in more detail later, but it is inevitable that this technology will be misused. Optimists may believe that short-term disadvantages are just an unfortunate prelude to the enormous social gains to follow, but when considering society's future, the extent to which we can influence it must be debated. Does it even make sense to ask 'What will the effect of microelectronics be on the future?' Is there really only one future or do we have a choice as to the future we want and the subsequent role of technology therein? For the industrialist's view of the next decade and the use of computers will differ fundamentally from, say, the considerations of a marxist, feminist, or ecologist.

Technology is not apolitical; the micro may be compared to a building block, which is itself neutral but when part of a working structure it reflects the desires and wishes of whoever designed or controls that system. Just as a wheel when part of a tractor is an entirely different entity from that seen on an armoured car, the micros inside missile guidance equipment bear no relationship to that controlling an intelligent wheelchair. The difference is at the macro, not micro, level.

An appreciation of the role of technology has led many individuals and organisations to consider how a society with devolved structures, limited growth, and low energy use can be achieved by the application of what has been called 'appropriate technologies'. Before considering whether the microchip is such a technology, it is necessary to relate, in general, the meaning of appropriate, and hence the final section of this chapter deals with a third and, to many, desirable hypothesis of the future.

1.3 APPROPRIATE TECHNOLOGIES

"Contemporary society is characterised by a growing distrust of technology. The many social benefits which technology has helped to bring about are being increasingly counterbalanced by the social problems associated with its use. These range from the oppression and manipulation of the individual to the widespread destruction of the natural environment and the depletion of the world's finite supply of natural resources. At the same time, man's technological skills have so far failed to provide effective solutions to many of the world's major problems, in particular those of mass poverty, starvation and international conflict. Technology is no longer seen as the omnipotent God that it was even ten years ago, . . ." (Dickson 1974).

The end of the 1970s furnished an opportunity for many commentators to give an 'in-depth' survey of the previous decade; one which saw the birth and coming-of-age of the microprocessor. Whereas the sixties had been a period of great technological optimism culminating in man's excursions to the moon, the seventies had witnessed many failures which tarnished the once widely held view that technology and science were the answer to all our problems. Schumacher, who was one of the first people to pinpoint the dangers of our present technologically based society, commented in his seminal book, *Small is Beautiful:*

"The modern industrial system, with all its intellectual sophistication, consumes the very bases on which it has been erected. To use the language of the economist, it lives on irreplaceable capital which it cheerfully treats as income. I specified three categories of such capital: fossil fuel, the tolerance margins of nature, and the human substance."

The fuel crisis, leading to expensive and scarce petrol, focused quite sharply the western nations' realisation that energy is neither cheap nor unlimited. Oil is not renewable; once it is used up it has gone for ever and hence conservation and conservative usage would appear to be the order of the day. Yet the United States appears to be blind to this position and continues to consume vast quantities of the world reserves.

Oil is but one resource; most industrial processes entail the transformation of a raw material into a manufactured product. Alas, few industries seriously consider recycling material, and it is therefore reasonable to assume that a continuing expansion in traditional manufacture will not go on indefinitely. Coupled with high industrial activity, excessive oil use, and modern agricultural activity comes the problem of pollution, with all its many facets. If there is one theme, above all others, that has dimmed the gleaming armour of modern technology then it is its effects upon the 'tolerance margins of nature'. It is true that such problems as city smog and river pollution are now showing signs of improvement, but with our ever increasing chemical and nuclear industries, who would wager that the 1990s will be pollution free?

The third element that Schumacher isolates is the effect on society as a whole of increased specialisation and centralisation. The essential message of *Small is Beautiful* is that small enterprises give more personalised control, provide more rewarding jobs, are more likely to produce socially necessary goods at a price available to everyone, and are less inclined to disrupt natural and social balances. The following two quotes highlight what many would call the unacceptable face of progress and technology:

> "There should be no place for machines that concentrate power in a few hands and turn the masses into mere machine minders, if indeed they do not make them unemployed." – Gandhi

> "They want production to be limited to useful things but they forget that the production of too many useful things results in too many useless people". – Karl Marx.

Other factors that have contributed to the growing dissatification with modern technology, of which microelectronics is now an intrinsic part, include its apparent inability to deal with the problems of the developing world. The green revolution was intended to end food shortages in large areas of the third world virtually overnight – it   failed almost completely. New high yield crop strains have proved to have low resistance to disease, and the cost of the required fertilisers and pesticides has placed an intolerable burden on local farmers, leaving them in a worse financial position than before.

United States' dissilusionment with the work of scientists and engineers has been attributed to the inability of powerful equipment to have any effect on the progress of the Vietnam war, which was lost despite (or possibly because of) the Americans' vast technological superiority. For many people in Britain, the Concorde fiasco has represented the summit of technical and international folly; as well as being unsaleable, unbelievably expensive to develop, and beyond the budget of ordinary air travellers, it has the amazing ability of using three times as much fuel as any other commercial aircraft – a rare achievement.

These are but a few of the many features of a modern industrial state that call into question the role of technology in our society:

> "Man had acquired formidable tools for refashioning his (sic) life before he had given the least thought to the question of what sort of life it would be well for him to fashion." Trevelyan (1946) – considering the first industrial revolution.

Present concern is focused upon three areas: nuclear power, genetic engineering, and microelectronics, all of which could have a profound effect on the future of our planet. Nuclear power is suffering from the 'three mile accident' syndrome and has emerged as a political issue in many western nations. Genetic engineering, although becoming increasingly widespread, has only recently been the subject of a self-imposed moratorium, and just one bad incident could turn public opinion strongly against it. As for microelectronics, the beginning of this chapter illustrates the divergent views associated with its envisaged role. Neither nuclear power nor genetic engineering is the subject of this book, but is it fair to cast microelectronics in the same mould? What type of technology does the micro really represent?

One way of categorising technology is to describe it as being either low, intermediate, or high; the criteria determining into which group any particular tool or system belongs is the capital cost per workplace necessary for its production. In 1970 this was generally agreed to imply that over £2000 per job defined a 'high-tec', whereas less than £1 meant that the technology was 'low'. Intermediate, as one might expect, falls between high and low but is usually expected to be somewhere between £20 and £200. Because of the large capital costs associated with electronics, it is clear into which group the micro falls.

1.3.1 Convivial Tools and Appropriate Technologies

"A student who can weave his (sic) technology into the fabric of society can claim to have had a liberal education. A student who cannot weave his technology into the fabric of society cannot even claim to be a good technologist." — Sir Eric Ashby.

There have been many names given to describe attempts at producing socially oriented technologies. Among the more common are: alternative technology, people's technology, soft technology, low-impact technology, liberatory technology and radical technology. Ivan Illich uses the term 'convivial' to describe a society that has a small, democratically controlled, technical, scientific, educational and political sector:

"Such a society, in which modern technologies serve politically interrelated individuals rather than managers, I will call 'convivial' . . . I have chosen 'convival' as a technical term to designate a modern society of responsibly limited tools." (Illich 1973).

This book hopes to present examples of how microelectronics could work as a convivial technology, in effect a third view of the future in which continuous exponential growth is not inevitable but made to reflect the genuine needs of society. Whether this view is any more valid than the optimistic or pessimistic one is not a function of the micro but of society itself.

The first and most important criterion of a convivial technology is that it must be generally accessible. One means of judging this is to compare the capital investment per workplace and the average wage of an able worker in that community. Accessibility is considered by many to exist only when these two factors are in approximate agreement. That is to say, if the average annual wage of an industrial worker is £5000 then this should be about the cost of his or her workplace. If the wage is considerably less than this, then new jobs will not be generated and there will be an unhealthy concentration of wealth in the society. In the developing world, where the average yearly wage is somewhat less then £100, high technology will spread to only a small section of the population –

"And this of course is precisely what has happened. Development has concentrated itself in cities, it has by-passed the great majority of people in the rural areas, and it has caused divisions in the society, far greater than would have occurred without the advent of such a technology." – (McRobie 1975).

For the third world then, appropriate technology is synonymous with inter-mediate technology; microelectronics has as yet no part to play in these societies, a point worth remembering when considering the production of the microchip (Chapter 4). Tools which would be more suitable for these communities are, for example, solar powered pumps, agricultural implements (not necessarily high-powered tractors), pedal power transport, simple batch process chemical production (caustic soda, soap etc) ferro-cement water storage, and local material building construction.

Rather than consider the cost of producing the technology, another way of examining its accessibility is to consider the price of the tool or service compared with the average wage. A measure of 'availability' here would be that the product could be bought by most working people, after one to two years' saving. An automatic washing machine, television, or stereo equipment therefore is more easily accessible in developed countries whereas the car, although popular, is not. In the third world, the position is entirely different with a year's saving only generating sufficient capital for perhaps a bicycle. In these communities there is the additional problem of widespread unemployment, and therefore the ability of a technology to generate jobs is as important as the goods produced. For this reason, the definition of accessibility normally takes these factors into account.

Criteria for Appropriateness
It is understandable that most of the effort that has gone into defining the criteria for appropriateness has concentrated on the very real problems of the developing nations. But the concept of an appropriate technology does not have to be associated with any particular level, for there are criteria which one would reasonably expect all technologies to encompass. De Wilde (1975) gives an extensive list, compiled by Frede Hvelplund of the School of Economics and Business Administration in Aarhus, Denmark, of the necessary criteria for defining Intermediate/Appropriate technologies. Within a developed nation, the following would at least be a minimal set of requirements.

1. The technology must be intelligible to the community as a whole.

2. It must be readily available at a price within the range of most individuals.

3. It must fulfil a socially useful purpose.

4. The tools and processes utilised must be under the maintenance and operational control of the local workforce.

5. It should use indigenous resources and skills.

6. It should create employment.

7. The production and use of the technology should present no health hazards to the personnel concerned.

8. It should be non-pollutant, ecologically sound, and where applicable it should recycle materials.

9. It must prevent external cultural domination.

10. It should where possible allow fulfilling, flexible, creative and innovatory use.

11. It should fit into the existing social infrastructure.

In short, an appropriate technology is one that is understood by the bulk of the population, uses skills which are readily available, does not adversely affect the environment or community, and which achieves a social objective. Technologies in our society which may be termed appropriate are: The telephone network (if it were somewhat cheaper), local bus and train services (if more accessible), domestic water supply (if environmental disturbances due to reservoirs could be minimised), and a number of energy sources, such as hydroelectric, geothermal, solar and wind. Whether wave power can be added to this list depends upon the extent to which the generating machinery is allowed to clutter coastal regions. Decidedly inappropriate technologies are to be found in all areas of a 'developed' society, as are many examples that fall between the two extremes.

The purpose of this book is firstly, to determine which tools within microelectronics can be termed 'convivial' and how they may be attained, and secondly, to present a set of criteria by which the probable consequences of technological applications can be judged — by so doing it is hoped that possible harmful effects may be averted. For though technology has been misused in the past, we must assume responsibility for restructuring it towards more socially acceptable ends. One drawback here is that technical planners, in general, lack a global perspective in which to view their work; designs need to reflect a true social awarness. To quote Schumacher once more:

"Man cannot live without science and technology any more than he can live against nature. What needs the most careful consideration, however, is the *direction* of scientific research. . . the direction should be towards non-violence rather than violence; towards an harmonious co-operation with nature rather than a warfare against nature; towards noiseless, low-energy, elegant and economical solutions normally applied in nature rather than the noisy, high-energy, brutal, wasteful, and clumsy solutions of our present-day sciences". (his italics) (Schumacher 1974)

2

The Evolution of the Microprocessor

Why is microelectronics having such a dramatic effect upon so many areas of our lives? The reasons are not difficult to understand but to give them some foundation, before going on to discuss ways of assessing actual applications, it would be worthwhile to look at computers in general and microcomputers in particular to pin-point exactly what they are, how they work and what they can do. One way of dealing with the question 'what is a computer?' is to look at its historical development and highlight the important features of a modern machine as they have emerged. One can then build up a conceptual model of a computer which is both easy to understand and sufficiently detailed to be of use to the non-specialist.

The modern computer can be seen to have evolved from a combination of three distinct fields, namely:

1. The development of calculating machines, dating from the 17th century.
2. The use of automation in the control of industrial processes, an early example of this is the Jacquard loom at the end of the 18th century.
3. The development of a branch of mathematics concerned with formal problem solving and logic. George Boole in the 19th century and Alan Turing in the early 20th century were two of the early contributors.

As with so many areas of technological advancement, the original stimulation arose from a combination or *convergence* of a number of hitherto distinct themes. In addition there were also a number of background developments which helped the birth of today's computer, such as electricity and the existence of switching apparatus in telephone exchanges. It is also important to realise that these three fields were themselves the result of countless other cultural activities. From the dawn of civilisation, men and women have faced problems of organising data and performing calculations, and to this end every society has endeavoured to develop number systems and practical aids to help in these tasks.

Undoubtedly the first and simplest calculating device is our fingers and, in extreme cases, our toes. Fingers cannot, however, be used as a method for storing numbers, this was probably first done by carving notches into pieces of wood or bone, examples of which have been found dating back over 30,000 years. These *Tally Sticks* as they are now called, became universally applied and were finally superseded by the use of paper and ink, a process which originated in China.

Another widespread method of representing numbers involved the tying of *knots* on cord, instances of which have been found in such diverse locations as Tibet and Peru. The Inca empire used an elaborate method of knot tying called *quipis* to record all official land transactions:

> "There is no doubt that this perhaps intentionally obscure manner of recording numbers, which only initiates could read was a strong support for the monarchial absolutism of the Inca ruler." (Menninger 1969).

It appears that information was power, even then.

Tally sticks and rope knots are primarily means of storing information, primitive aids to calculation usually involved the use of pebbles arranged in groups on a purpose-built *counting board*[†]. It is uncertain where or when the first counting board was constructed upon which the pebbles or counters remain fixed, but the resulting device which we call an *abacus* has, for more than three thousand years, been the most appropriate tool for the 'doing of arithmetic'.

Although the abacus became extensively used in Asia, for Europe the most popular tool, particularly for the engineer, has been the *slide rule*. It appeared in about 1630 and was generally appreciated for the way in which it automated the tedious tasks of multiplication and division. The slide rule, where numerical values are associated with length, was a direct result of John Napier's work on logarithms published in 1614.

2.1 THE EARLY MACHINES – FUNDAMENTALS OF A COMPUTER

In the 17th and 18th centuries as commerce and society became more 'sophisticated', the ancient calculating tools and aids proved inadequate. Society was now in the mechanical era and a number of attempts were made to build calculating machines, the two most famous contributions being made by Pascal (1623-62) and Leibniz (1646-1716).

[†] The word 'calculation' derives from the Latin *calculi* meaning 'small pebbles'.

Most of the early attempts at automation were centred on the weaving industry,. Basile Boughon is credited with inventing, in 1725, the idea of using a perforated tape to control the production of ornamental patterns; the holes indicated which warp thread was to be used for each pass of the shuttle (Usher 1954). Boughon's ideas were later improved by Falcon, a master silk weaver from Lyon, France, and again by Vavcanson who, in 1750, designed a completely automated draw loom.

Although Vavcanson had the ideas, it was left to Jacquard to put them into practice and by so doing produce a really successful, widely used draw loom. His system used a set of linked perforated cards which passed continuously over mechanical sensors, a process that was subsequently taken up by the computer pioneers, Babbage and Hollerith; the paper tape and punched card systems of modern computers were a direct analogy to Jacquard's method. But as well as giving a mechanism by which data could be entered into calculating machines, automation provided an important conceptual model, namely that large complicated problems could be broken down into a sequence of smaller, simpler steps — the essence of computer programming.

2.1.1 Babbage and Lovelace

It is rare in any historical account to be able to say, with confidence, exactly where and when an important chain of events began; and yet Babbage's Analytical Engine, although never completed, is universally accepted as the world's first computer. Its basic design is as good a model of a computer as one might wish and there is only one critical area in which it falls down. Charles Babbage (1791-1871), the son of a wealthy banker, was the founder of the Analytical Society in Cambridge and holder of the Lucasian Chair of Mathematics at that university, he also took an active interest in such diverse fields as dynamometer measurement of railways, pin manufacture, actuarial 'life tables' and politics — standing for Parliament on one occasion.

Ada Augusta, Countess of Lovelace (1815-52) was the only child of Lord and Lady Byron. She studied mathematics under Mary Somerville, a famous teacher of the time, and had shown a particular gift for this subject as well as languages. At the time of Babbage's major work she was one of the few people to actually understand his ideas and worked closely with him on various aspects of his Analytical Engine, making considerable contributions herself, especially in the area that we now call programming.

The Difference Engine

Although the life and times of Babbage and Lovelace are of great interest (Moseley 1964), for our purposes attention must be limited to his two calculating engines. In the preparation of mathematical tables, which was a major nineteenth century activity, it is usual to calculate exact values from the fundamental mathematical relationships at only a limited number of what are termed *pivotal values,* intermediate points being calculated from the pivotal ones by interpolation. One means of achieving interpolation, particularly for polynomial functions, involves the comparison of successive pivotal points and is known as the *method of differences.*

Whilst a student at Cambridge, Babbage had conceived the idea of building a machine, or engine as he called it, which would automatically produce mathematical tables by the method of difference. He built a small scale model to demonstrate his principle and in 1823 gained financial support from the British Government to the tune of £17,000. Even with this substantial backing Babbage could not complete his engine, due mainly to technical problems, disagreements with the builder and his own increasing lack of interest in the project. The Government's financial support was withdrawn in 1842. Some years later, a Swedish engineer George Scheutz, successfully completed a difference engine based on Babbage's ideas, a copy of which was bought by the British Government in 1864.

The Analytical Engine

Although of interest, the difference engine was special-purpose device and its value was really only that of a springboard, propelling Babbage towards the concept of a general-purpose automatic calculating machine:

> ". . .it appears that the whole of the conditions which enable a *finite* machine to make calculations of *unlimited* extent are fulfilled in the Analytical Engine. . . I have converted the infinity of space, which was required by the conditions of the problem into the infinity of time." (his italics) (Babbage 1864).

The Analytical Engine,[†] like its predecessor, was never completed, the precision machinery it required was too advanced for his time. Therefore all we know of the engine comes from an account by Lady Lovelace[††] and some unpublished notes and drawings by Babbage himself (Babbage 1837). He apparently envisaged the complete machine to consist of the following parts:

1. Two *control* input devices. The action of the complete engine was to be controlled by two sets of Jacquard style *operation cards*; the operations available were as follows:

   (i)   addition of two numbers
   (ii) subtraction of two numbers
   (iii) multiplication of two numbers

[†] A detailed description of this machine is given by Wilkes (1977).

[††] In 1840, Babbage was invited to a meeting in Turin; L. F. Menabrea a young engineer in the audience published an account of Babbage's ideas in 1842; Lady Lovelace translated this paper and added extensive notes of her own (three times the original). This was published in Taylor's Scientific Memoirs in 1843.

(iv) multiplication of two numbers to a given number of figures

(v) division of one number by another

(vi) division of one number by another limited to a given number of figures in the quotient

Two sets of cards were to be used, one to deal with the calculations to be performed and the other, the variable cards, were associated with the control of data through the engine. Together, these would now be recognised as constituents of a computer program.

2. A further Jacquard input device for use with data.

3. A *barrel* was used to control the operation of the engine. Cards would be 'advanced' under the direction of the barrel which, having received an instruction, would perform the sub-operations required through its collection of vertical stops. In modern jargon, the barrel is equivalent to the *control unit* and the vertical stops represent a primitive form of *micro-instruction.*

4. A *store* for holding numbers, both those forming the initial data and the subsequent intermediate values calculated during the operation. The store was intended to be made up of cogged wheels, one per decimal digit on a vertical shaft and was to accommodate one thousand numbers, each being represented by up to fifty decimal places! Numbers were transferred by an elaborate mechanism of gears and rods.

5. Secondary storage was furnished by *number cards.* If the store was getting too full or if intermediate values needed to be permanently recorded, the engine would automatically punch the required cards which could then be re-read. By providing this facility, Babbage ensured that 'calculations of unlimited extent are fulfilled in the Analytical Engine.'

6. The core of the machine was the *mill* in which the arithmetic operations took place, these were either addition, subtraction, multiplication, division or the extraction of roots. The logical problems involved in doing arithmetic on a machine with a fifty decimal place accuracy occupied Babbage for some considerable time. He appears to have derived a number of efficient algorithms which were to be incorporated in the mill.

7. Finally, there were to be a number of output devices including a card punch, quick printer – using carbonised paper – and a finer, slower copper-plate printer. He also apparently considered attaching an automatic curve drawing machine, anticipating the need for graph plotting equipment on modern computers.

Schematic View of a Computer

Although Babbage's machine is of historical interest, the main reason for studying
its structure here is to illustrate a simple model of a computer, a model which
serves to describe modern machines as well as the Analytical Engine. Fig. 2.1 is a
schematic picture of Babbage's Engine using modern terminology. The main

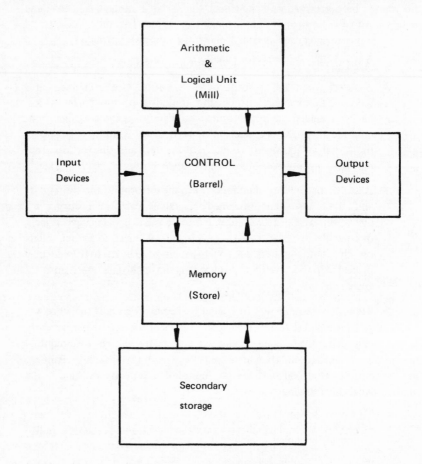

Fig. 2.1 — A simple view of a computer

property of this and all other computers is its generality of function; it does not
just do one type of calculation but will take its instructions from the user. In a
functional sense all the computer does is to act upon data to produce results,
therefore two of the most important devices are those concerned with input
and output; whether these be a Jacquard type card reader or a visual display
unit is of secondary importance.

Another essential element of any computer is the store, or *memory* as it is called today. During any calculation temporary values will be generated and these must be held by the computer for future use. One of the most fascinating features of Babbage's work is his realisation that the storage of information is a distinct activity warranting its own dedicated machinery. With any computer, no matter how large, there comes a time when all the intermediate memory is exhausted and it becomes necessary to add a form of *secondary storage,* capable of holding unlimited quantities of data. For the Analytical Engine, Babbage used Jacquard cards, modern machines now use magnetic discs and tapes. To be accurate Babbage did not appear to draw any distinction between initial data and temporary values, because they both had to be input to the store by the same apparatus.

In keeping with Babbage's compartmentalised view of his machine, the arithmetic operations were undertaken in a special device, the mill. This is again a structure to be found on all large computers where fast operating arithmetic and logical electronics are isolated into one unit. Finally, there comes the question of controlling the whole process. If input, output, storage and calculation are to be undertaken by different sections of the machine then the flow of data must be controlled centrally. This action, assigned to the barrel on the Analytical Engine, is now said to be performed by the *central processor unit* or CPU, which if contained on a single chip of silicon is called a microprocessor. The function of the CPU is to interpret the instructions given to the computer and to instigate the step by step action which will cause any instruction to be obeyed.

In addition to the difficulties in designing and constructing the actual engine, there is the matter of how to split up the mathematical problems into a sequence of elementary instructions which can then be dealt with automatically. It was this area with which Ada Lovelace was most concerned. She highlighted many of the logical difficulties associated with this process and illustrated her findings by describing several procedures for dealing with quite advanced mathematical calculations.

Babbage's Heritage

"In writing of Babbage as a computer pioneer one must at once admit that his work, however brilliant and original, was without influence on the modern developments of computers." (Wilkes 1977)

The reasons for this unfortunate situation are numerous; the engine was never finished nor even neared completion; Babbage almost completely failed to communicate his ideas because of his growing disenchantment with society in general; Ada Lovelace, although she understood his work, appreciated its value and attempted to write extensively about it, died at the age of thirty-seven before she had managed to give a complete description. Above all, the main reason must be that there was little need for a machine of such sophistication at that time. His Difference Engine would have had a use, if completed, as did

Scheutz's, but the Analytical Engine would have to wait nearly a century before its time arrived. Babbage summed up his own efforts in his book, 'Passages from the Life of a Philosopher':

> "If, unwarranted by my example, any man (sic) shall undertake and shall succeed in really constructing an engine embodying in itself the whole of the executive department of mathematical analysis upon different principles or by simpler mechanical means, I have no fear of leaving my reputation in his charge, for he alone will be fully able to appreciate the nature of my efforts and the value of their results."

2.1.2 The First Electronic Computer

Seventy years after Babbage's death, his dream came true when Konrad Zuse built his Z3 machine, which is believed to be the first general purpose, program controlled electro-mechanical computer. This isolated development in Germany, like Babbage's work, was destined to have little effect on the evolution of the modern computer. For in the US, interest was already being shown at Harvard university, Bell Laboratories and Iowa State College (now a university). From this work the world's first electronic computer emerged.

ENIAC

The initial stimulus for the ENIAC project came from John Mauchly who, in August 1942, prepared a memorandum entitled 'The Use of High Speed Vacuum Tube Devices for Calculating'. For those unfamiliar with the structure of a valve (also known as a vacuum tube) a diagram is given in Fig. 2.2. A valve is essentially an amplifier, pumping electrons through a vacuum from a heated electrode; they normally measure about 3 inches in height. The decision to build an electronic device was finally taken on the 2nd April 1943, when an agreement was reached between Moore School and the Ballistic Research Laboratory. Work began in May that year and ENIAC (Electronic Numerical Integrator and Calculator) was finally assembled in the autumn of 1945, with a formal dedication ceremony taking place at Moore School on 1st February 1946.

ENIAC occupied 3000 cubic feet, weighed 30 tons, contained 18,000 vacuum tubes and consumed 200 kilowatts of electric power but it could add two numbers together in under 3 milliseconds and multiply them in 2,800, which was a considerable improvement over its electromechanical predecessors. Internally ENIAC had a number of features which we would recognise in a computer today, including a central clock to synchronise operation and the use of flip-flops as the basic memory element. Re-programming ENIAC was possible, though difficult, and although it was originally envisaged as a giant calculator it deserves to be described as general-purpose. In other ways ENIAC was very primitive, had a low storage capacity and lacked a truly binary structure. Even before it was completed its designers were looking towards the next computer in which they hoped to eradicate many of the logical difficulties that had arisen in the initial construction.

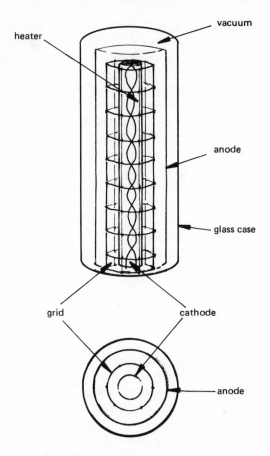

Fig. 2.2 — A Triode. By altering the voltage on the grid, the passage of electrons from the heated cathode to the anode is controlled to give a two state device.

2.1.3 The Stored Program Computer

There remains one further feature needed to complete the description of a modern computer. So far all the machines discussed have been programmable in the sense that different sets of instructions could facilitate alternative operations, but the required instructions had to be fed individually into the control unit, using an outside medium such as a paper tape. Because the reading of a tape is inevitably slower than the electronic action of the computer itself, the overall speed of the operation was limited to that of the input peripherals.

It is understandable that the major emphasis in constructing the early computers was of actually piecing together all of the valves and associated circuitry so that a working machine could be demonstrated. Once this had been achieved, or at least thought out, more detailed attention could be paid to some of the actual processes employed. Because only two state devices are feasible with electronic components, it is obvious that binary arithmetic is the most appropriate to use internally. Many of the early machines, including ENIAC, used a variety of decimal codes in an attempt to stay with this familiar system though unfortunately this tended to introduce more difficulties than it resolved.

In the construction of a machine containing 18,000 valves there are considerable perplexities in planning the overall design. Fortunately a branch of mathematics known as Boolean Algebra which dates back to 1845 and deals with systems containing only two states, was available. In 1938, Claude Shannon demonstrated that Boole's algebra could be applied to switching and relay circuits, thereby transforming the problems of design from electronics to algebra (Shannon 1938). Extensive work has subsequently been done on this algebra and one can now deal with the most detailed aspects of computer architecture and operation without ever having to revert to questions of voltage, resistance or capacitance etc. A computer is better understood by considering it to be a logical, rather than an electrical machine.

The problems of a slow input device appear to have a dawned upon the ENIAC workers, whilst they were attempting to deal with some of the consequences of limited storage; one way around the difficulty of slow input is to read all the instructions in at one time, store them as data and then operate on the instructions one at a time in the usual way. It is many thousand times quicker to read an instruction from valve storage than via a paper tape reader.

By the time the idea of stored programs and homogeneous memory (capable of holding data and instructions) had crystallised it was too late to alter the design of ENIAC. It was decided to construct a further machine, the EDVAC (Electronic Discrete Variable Automatic Computer) to incorporate this new approach. Work was started on this project in 1946 but progressed slowly, the machine only becoming operational in 1951. Because of this, the distinction of being the world's first electronic, stored program, general purpose, digital computer fell to a British development, the EDSAC (Electronic Delay Storage Automatic Calculator), which was built at Cambridge under the leadership of Professor M. Wilkes and became operational in May 1949.[†]

2.1.4 The Internal Operation of a Computer

In Fig. 2.1 a schematic diagram of a computer was presented in which the controlling instructions were given to the central processor from outside. By 1950 this had changed; complete sets of instructions were issued in advance to the computer as data, to be stored in memory and then transferred to the processor as required. This facility, coupled with our basic design, gives the following description of

[†]There is evidence that an experimental computer at Manchester University actually ran a stored program before this date – see Lavington (1980).

a 'generic computer' — one that is as appropriate today as it was 30 years ago and which applies equally to the largest IBM giant and the smallest microcomputer:

1. They accept alphabetic or numeric data from the outside world; typical media being punched cards, paper tape, magnetic tape, keyboards, electronic measuring devices and, in the near future, direct voice recognition.

2. They store data electromagnetically.

3. They can manipulate this data to produce new information.

4. The instructions for manipulating this data can also be stored electromagnetically.

5. They transmit, manipulate and store data digitally and in binary form.

6. They output results, to line printer paper, magnetic and paper tape, visual display units, electrical control apparatus and, in the long term, via voice synthesis.

The 'power' of a computer derives from storing data digitally for accuracy and electronically for speed. Since 1950, technology has advanced and now offers even greater reliability and cheaper equipment which can hold more data and manipulate it faster; but the basic structure as outlined above, is still applicable. Once the idea of storing the instructions was accepted, it became increasingly significant that the instructions given be both correct, in terms of doing what was required, and efficient, in the sense of doing the job with the fewest computer operations.

2.2 TECHNOLOGICAL ADVANCEMENTS : THE FOUR GENERATIONS

Although in one sense computers have changed little since the 1950's, there is an immense difference between todays' machines and those of only thirty years ago. In attempting to compare the performance of alternative computer systems, be they contemporaries or not, one must define operating parameters which can be applied across the board to all such systems. Capital cost, delivery data, maintenance cost, staff requirement, reliability and ease of use are some of the more general topics of interest. They reflect the external construction but do not give the precise information needed to present a detailed description. Criteria relevant to this type of analysis could be:

(a) The type of technology from which the central processor is constructed.

(b) The speed at which such technology works.
(c) The speed at which an item of data can be written to, or read from, the primary memory — *access time.*
(e) The size of memory available on the system.
(f) The forms of secondary storage offered.

It is customary, when discussing the growth of the computer industry, to talk in terms of 'generations', both as a form of simplification and to highlight the major technological advances that have taken place. The concept of a generation is inevitably vague and there is therefore some controversy about exactly how many generations there have been, when they start and finish and what actually defines each one. Although there is, unavoidably, some overlap the following dates can be given as an indication of the time scales involved:

1st Generation — 1945-1954 : Valve Computers
2nd Generation — 1954-1965 : Transistors
3rd Generation — 1965-   : Integrated Circuits
4th Generation — 1972-   : LSI

The 3rd and 4th generations represent the computer technology in operation today, and are therefore of greatest interest to us here.

2.2.1 The 3rd Generation — Integrated Circuits

No sooner had the first transistor been manufactured than it became clear that this was not the end of miniaturisation but a mere overture to the technological performance to come. Although transistors themselves were made increasingly smaller, the difficulty of interconnecting them remained and it became apparent that rather than miniaturise individual transistors, it would be more efficient to design complete logical units on one piece of silicon. A number of transistors, with their associated circuitry and connections, could therefore be collected together upon a single *chip* of semiconductor material, thereby reducing the size of the unit whilst simultaneously simplifying the construction of computer circuits. At first, because of technical difficulties, only a small number of components (between 20 and 50) were placed on a single chip. These were then organised into modules which could be tested and easily replaced in order to increase reliability. A single operation in this type of technology can be performed in a mere 100 nanoseconds.[†]

Other features of the third generation machine were the increased amount of magnetic core memory used, the deployment of magnetic discs, drums and tapes, and the use of extended core for secondary storage. Additionally, multi-programming direct-access methods of communicating with the computer were becoming increasingly commonplace. Direct access implies the use of a visual

[†] A nanosecond is a thousand millionth of a second (0.000000001 sec).

display unit with keyboard to converse directly with the computer. In a normal installation there are, perhaps, a hundred such VDUs all 'talking' directly and all needing instant dialogue. The *operating system*[††] which allows many users to access the computer, apparently simultaneously, is called *multiprogrammable*. Most modern large computers, or *mainframes* as they are more commonly known, are of this type and are therefore of the 3rd generation. In Fig. 2.3 a hypothetical installation is shown, including a number of *peripherals*, full descriptions of which can be found in Meek (1977).

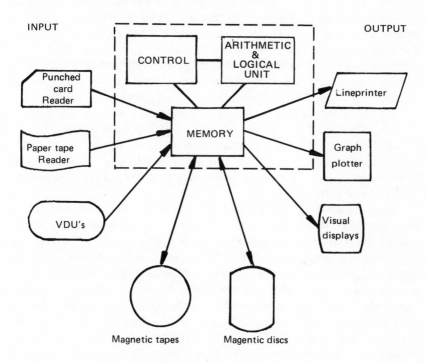

Fig. 2.3 – A typical mainframe computer system.

2.2.2 The 4th Generation – LSI
The distinction between 3rd and 4th generation computers is less clear, with many preferring to label the 4th generation as 'late-third'. An integrated circuit, as we have seen, contains a number of components on a single chip of semi-conductor material; the greater the number of components, the fewer the chips required for any particular product. Therefore, the manufacturers continued to squeeze

††The operating system is the package of standard programs that enables the user to work easily with the machine; for a large machine the operating system could contain over one million program statements.

as much circuitry as possible onto each individual chip, until eventually the stage was reached whereby a complete computer, or at least the important processor part, could be fitted onto a single chip. The microprocessor or LSI (large scale integrator) had arrived. Although an LSI is purely a progression from an integral circuit, its scale of operation and the subsequent barrage of applications for this one-chip-processor makes it as different from 3rd generation technology as was the transistor from the valve; it rightly has a generation tag of its own.

The first commercially available microprocessor, the Intel 4004, was available in 1971. It comprised some 1600 transistors on a slab of silicon less than 0.25 sq cms in area, but in many ways this first product was very limited. The greatest integer which could be held was 15, because the 4004 was a four bit machine; that is to say it allocated only four binary digits to each item of data. Eight bit processor part, could be fitted upon a single chip. The microprocessor or LSI recently, the sixteen bit micro has become available giving a word length[†] comparable with medium sized machines or minicomputers.

The processor, although the most important component of a computer, is not the only one of significance. Memory chips which are also a product of miniaturisation are, though somewhat more mundane, equally responsible for the 'micro revolution'. In 1979 the first 64K[††] RAM memory was announced, with this chip measuring a mere 0.5 sq cms; access time for any item of data is in the order of 100 nanoseconds.

The term RAM signifies the kind of memory, for there are two basic types, ROM and RAM. ROM — Read Only Memory — is, as its name implies, capable only of giving out information; new data cannot be placed on the chip whilst it is on the computer but must be 'burnt on' either at manufacture or in special laboratory equipment. One vital property of ROM is that the information it holds is not destroyed when the power is switched off, but will remain to be reused when the computer is turned on again. By comparison, the other type of memory is wiped clean by switching off the machine and can have new data placed on it at any time. This is called RAM — Random Access Memory. Though this name is somewhat misleading, random access means that any item of data on the chip can be read in the same time interval, no matter where it is located. The opposite of random access is 'serial access'; an example of this is a magnetic tape where it would take longer to retrieve data from the end of the tape than from the beginning. The confusion between the two types of memory arises because ROM is also random access; a better name for RAM to distinguish if from read only is RWM — Read/Write Memory.

The term microcomputer is now in common use and yet what it implies, a processor and adequate memory storage on a single chip, does not yet exist.

[†] In most computers, storage is allocated in groups of bits called 'words', the PDP range of minicomputers has a word length of 16, the IBM 370 — 32 and the ICL 2980 — 64.

[††] 1K = 1024 separate binary memory locations.

Microprocessors do have some memory on them but this is usually insufficient. The present usage of the word 'microcomputer' is taken to mean a collection of chips, one being the processor, a few being memory units, and some others are usually specialised chips dealing with input, output and perhaps arithmetic functions. All these elements of electronic miniaturisation are mounted onto a single, or a collection of, *circuit boards* which facilitate connections between the different elements and the external devices. A typical set of circuit boards would have forty-eight 1K RAM memory chips, one 4K ROM, one processor with arithmetic/ logic unit, a disc drive controller and a VDU interface. The ROM unit might contain information on how the system should start up when power is switched on, or, if the microcomputer is controlling some industrial process, it might contain permanently stored sets of operating instructions. Although this is a very simple layout of a circuit board there is, nevertheless, a significant similarity between this and the schematic view of Babbage's machine given in Fig. 2.1 — confirmation that computers are, at this level, very straightforward logic machines.

Microelectronics is an unusual technology in that it can be understood at a number of different levels. No tool or equipment should ever be seen by its users as purely a 'black-box' whose inner operations are a complete mystery. On the other hand, to completely understand the behaviour of semiconductor material, a knowledge of atomic theory and crystal structure of a highly detailed nature is required. The conceptual view of a computer developed in this chapter has cut between these extremes to present a model of computer operations which is appropriate for most users, though devoid of complicated details. Even so, many technical readers will wish to examine in more depth exactly what chips are and how they are made. For such people there are a number of descriptive articles in popular magazines, such as Sutton (1979) in the New Scientist. In simple terms, the manufacturing process involves the following stages:

1. Research and Development.
2. Fabrication — (setting of the chip from a master mask).
3. Assembly — (mounting and wiring).
4. Testing.

2.2.3 A Typical Microcomputer System

Having dealt with the inner structure of the micro, user equipment will now be considered. A microcomputer is based on a LSI processor, memory and input/ output chips. At the heart of any such computer is the circuit board (or boards) and the bulky power supply which converts mains electricity into the requirements of the minute chip circuitry. Unlike the few mainframe computer manufacturers, there are many hundreds of different microcomputer manufacturers competing to sell these systems, although the processor on which the different machines are based is normally only one of a range of three or four popular models. A number of the cheaper type of microcomputers are aimed at the enthusiast and have been given the label 'Personal Computer', but to do any effective work, particularly in data processing, the following equipment is essential:

1. *Microcomputer with at least 32K of memory.* For laboratory work it should have an IEEE-488 'bus' connection and for all uses there should be series and parallel ports available.[†]

2. *Keyboard of standard type* preferably with a numerical pad.

3. *Screen for display* — many microcomputer systems have keyboard, screen and processor all in one case, others combine the circuit board with the keyboard and then require the user to plug in an ordinary TV, which opens up the possibility of colour display but can be very tiring on the eyes.

4. *Printer with full character set* — as good a quality as possible. Speed is not usually as critical a factor with this type of application as is the noise of operation!

5. *Floppy disc secondary storage.* This is the type of disc commonly used with microcomputers, the discs are either 5 or 8 inches across and usually fit into a dual drive. A 5 inch single density, single sided system will hold approximately 80,000 characters of data per drive; the 8 inch dual density double sided will store 1 million characters.

In many ways the secondary storage is the all important factor; some microcomputer systems use a standard cassette player and tapes to hold data but this operation is very slow and rarely suitable for anything but the transfer of information from one computer to another. With floppy discs it is important that the right system be purchased so that the data requirement will fit onto a reasonably manageable number of discs. One disadvantage of the floppy disc arrangement is that it is not entirely reliable and it is therefore always advisable to hold backup copies of all important discs. The term 'floppy' arrives from comparisons with the traditional, established hard discs which are far more reliable and hold considerably more data (typical small unit might hold 5 million characters). But these latter are also more expensive, so much so that only recently, as their price has fallen, can they be found on micro systems.

The price of the above collection varies but would be of the order of £3000-£4000; this could become cheaper but the expensive items are really the printer

---

[†] A 'port' is a connection by which peripheral devices may be linked to the microcomputer, series implies that only single 'bits' of data can pass at one time through this connection, parallel means that 8 bits can pass simultaneously.

and the disc unit, whose price will not fall sharply because they incorporate moving mechanical parts. A simple microcomputer with only a keyboard and screen is already available at under £600.

The future will probably bring a number of alterations, most of which could be economically advantageous to the user but might not significantly change the basic structure of the equipment. One exception will be the opportunity to link such systems together via telephone lines, not only will this open a medium of communications between microcomputers but it will allow small systems to interact with large computers containing extensive data banks. Economically the microcomputer and mainframe are worlds apart (£3000 against £1 million), so it is not surprising that the micro, having evolved from the large machine, is now a direct competitor.

2.3 HARDWARE AND SOFTWARE — THE CRITICAL DISTINCTION

Two of the more common terms used in this unfortunately jargon-ridden technology are *hardware* and *software*. Hardware is the physical apparatus, the semiconductor chips, the wiring, the connections etc. These are the rigid permanent entities, the development of which was considered in the last section. Hardware in itself, however, can accomplish nothing; instructions must be given to the processor if it is to be anything other than an expensive ornament. Software is the term used to indicate these instructions and it is the linking of the commands into what are termed programs which turn the inert machine into a potentially useful device. Even if a microcomputer takes its instructions from a ROM memory, this program would still have been created outside the computer.

Why is it that sophisticated computer equipment requires software to tell it what to do? After all, many more mundane electrical devices such as light bulbs, electric kettles and vacuum cleaners have a well defined function dictated by their structure, thereby eradicating any need for software. Other electrical equipment such as a television allows the user to choose the channel she or he wishes to watch. It would make no sense to have separate television sets for each channel because the same electrical components will do for all stations. Similarly we only have one radio which we can use to listen to a large variety of broadcasts, as long as instructions are given as to which particular wavelength is required.

TVs and radios are therefore, in a sense, general purpose devices. Even televisions with different screen sizes will have a large number of common internal components. The reason for this is straightforward economics; the more uses a device has, the greater will be the number produced and the cheaper each copy becomes. This analysis applies particularly to the microelectronics industry. One can manufacture a chip which will perform the control requirements of, for example, an automatic washing machine; similarly, one could be produced to control the operation of a camera. Both of these applications would attract sales, and if one could use the same microelectronic mechanism for both these applications and many thousands of others besides, then the basic chip component could be mass produced by the million with the result that its low cost would be reflected by high sales. In order for the basic microprocessor to be flexible enough to accommodate a variety of functions it needs to be adaptable, but without altering its actual hardware structure. The microprocessor has therefore followed its ancestors by being programmable.

A number of important distinctions can be drawn between the nature of hardware and software; one of the most significant is that whereas individuals cannot make microprocessors, they can program microcomputers. Although there are a small number of mainly international companies which manufacture the raw material in the form of chip components, the development of this raw material into a useful aid or tool is NOT under their control but in the hands of the user. Knowledge of the basic concepts of computer architecture is always useful, but more important is an appreciation of what programming involves. With an understanding of programming techniques, individuals or small organisations can adapt or modify microcomputer incorporated apparatus to their own particular needs. Examples of this will be given in Chapter 5.

The nature of the split between hardware and software is further reflected by the commercial price paid for each. Because of their 'basic commodity' nature and mass production, the microprocessor chip costs only a few pounds and other chips are available at less than 50p (less than one US dollar); this is in comparison to the thousands if not millions of pounds that the large, older computers cost. Software, however, has not witnessed this revolution; in fact charges for the one-off program have risen considerably since the 1960s. Whilst mass sales of some types of software could greatly reduce their cost, these would tend to be the more general purpose programs such as a language or an operating system. One example of this is the way the price of the language BASIC has fallen from over £2000, when specifically designed for a minicomputer, to less than £7 for the micros of today. In future, many standardized business packages which sell widely will show a similar fall in price.

The value of a piece of hardware lies in its reliability and low capital cost, whereas the strength of the software depends upon its flexibility. Software can be modified to accommodate local requirements and future developments, for even though a computer program is running efficiently and fulfilling its design specifications, it is never static. Changes will be needed in order to include new tasks and this ability of allowing the user to develop or manipulate the software gives the microcomputer so much power as a general purpose tool.

Innovations such as computer systems which produced their own software, raise alarming questions not only about programmer employment but also about the credibility of information originating from a computer whose operation no one, not even the programmer, understands. Professor D. Michie of the Department of Machine Intelligence at Edinburgh University considers it imperative that in complicated situations, *expert systems* be developed which are not only structured towards human needs but also incorporate a *human window* so that any analysis undertakén by the computer can be questioned (Michie 1980). Only in this way can it be guaranteed that the user remain in control of the system and not the other way round.

Represented in the term 'software' are a number of techniques which can be expressed in a variety of different programming languages, for just as the hardware of a modern computer has evolved from its 1940s pattern, programming has also progressed from its simple beginnings. As an introduction to modern techniques it is both interesting and of value to trace the historical growth of the software facilities currently available to the programmer.

2.3.1 The Development of Programming

Designers of the early computers tried to create a machine which could accomplish a number of different tasks. In the earliest computers this was achieved in a cumbersome fashion as the machine needed to be rewired in order to run a new set of instructions. Most of the people involved in the construction of these early models were primarily concerned with mechanical aspects, i.e. getting them to work, rather than with the conceptual difficulties of problem solving.

By 1952 computers had a basic vocabulary of some 29 operations (Goldstine 1972) and could store programs using these compounds. A typical program calculating an addition would look like:

```
0.   00000010101111001010
1.   00000010111111001000
2.   00000011001110101000
3.   00000010101111001100
4.   00000010111111000110
5.   00000011001111001000
6.   00000011001110101000
```

While this is exactly what the computer 'understands' it is virtually unintelligible to a human. A single instruction from this machine was made up of two parts. The first ten binary digits correspond to the *address* of some single item of data. This datum is either to be used by the instruction or alternatively the result of some calculation is to be *stored* at this address. The second ten binary digits indicate the task to be performed, an addition or subtraction etc. This series of digits constitutes a program which the computer can interpret directly and is therefore termed a *machine language* program, but because it is virtually impossible to use this long winded format without human error, *symbolic languages* were constructed to simplify matters. An instruction in this language would have, for example, a decimal address section and an mnemonically coded operation part. In such a form, the previous could now be presented as:

0.	10	L	Load 'A' from address 10
1.	11	A	Add to 'A' contents of 11
2.	12	S	Store this value at 12
3.	10	R	Reload 'A'
4.	11	X	Multiply by contents of 11
5.	12	A	Add in the value of 12
6.	12	S	Store this value at 12

If the value of X is stored at address 10 and the value of Y at 11, then this program is calculating

$$X + Y + XY$$

and storing the result at address 12. This symbolic language, although readable to the programmer, needs to be converted into a machine language program and entered into the computer. Originally this was performed manually but 'loading' programs were later developed to automate this process.

Modern computers and microprocessors can still be programmed in this way. Rather than a symbolic code, an *assembly language* is used and this has a similar form. Programs written in assembly language are converted into machine code by a program called an *assembler*. Instead of 29 basic operations, the modern Z80 microprocessor has 158. The advantage of writing programs in assembly language is that one is very close to the operation of the machine and it is therefore possible to produce efficient coding, which is of particular importance where speed constraints are critical. The disadvantages, however, stem from precisely the same properties. One has to know the processor very well before it can be programmed effectively if, indeed, at all. Different computers have their own assembly languages and hence it is not possible to transfer programs from one type of computer to another. Moreover, although a symbolic type of language is an immense improvement on machine codes, it still has a rather unnatural form in that it fails to reflect the manner in which we conceptualise problems. For these reasons considerable efforts have been focused upon the development of *High Level Languages*.

In these languages, solutions to problems are specified in a way more natural for humans, and more related to the terminology used in the problem area, be it mathematical or commercial, and little or no knowledge of the actual computer is required. Surprisingly, one of the first such languages developed — FORTRAN (FORmula TRANslator) — is still the most popular one in use in the scientific community; unfortunately this reflects more upon programmers' unwillingness to change than on the qualities of the language. There is also the problem of the personal and financial investment already laid out in existing programs. FORTRAN first evolved between 1954 and 1956 for use on the IBM

704 computer and has been backed by IBM ever since. It sustained a number of modifications before being standardised as FORTRAN IV in 1966; more recently an improved version, FORTRAN 77, has become available. Following on from FORTRAN, there have been a large number of languages developed, including ALGOL 60 and ALGOL 68, LISP, PL1, SIMULA and the widely used commercial language COBOL.

One particularly straightforward language which can be found on most microcomputers is BASIC (Beginners All-purpose Symbolic Instruction Code). As its name suggests, this is a simple (though nonetheless high level) language, which has enabled users from many disciplines to write their own programs. Although BASIC offers some attractive features, such as the ability to handle text as data, it suffers from a number of shortcomings which are exacerbated in more complex programs. As an alternative, therefore, Pascal[†] is becoming increasingly popular on microcomputers, as well as on mainframes. Pascal was designed by Niklaus Wirth in late 1960s, primarily as a teaching language and as such it is extensively used, especially by the Computer Science departments in many universities. As a language Pascal has a larger vocabulary than its predecessors but, although it is more difficult to learn, its structure furnishes the user with a greater selection of programming tools. The richer the language is, the more rewarding its use will be.

What languages will the future bring? The fashion of designing new languages, which was very popular in the sixties, is on the decline, just as the practice by universities of building their own computers was soon superseded by the development of standard manufactured models. One exception to this is to the new language Ada (after Ada Lovelace, a co-worker with Charles Babbage on that first computer). This has been developed from sponsorship by the American Department of Defence, in response to the need to have a high level language which will function on multiple computer systems, possibly incorporating both large and small computers, as well as on single processors. In particular the requirements of a language that would give *parallel processing*[††] in *embedded systems* were paramount. As with so many areas in computing, the initial stimulus and finance has come from 'defence' expenditure. The American authorities established a list of requirements in 1975 and, after examining existing languages and finding them seriously lacking, a specification for a new language was announced (Pyle 1979). After competition by a number of groups, and a series of refinements to the specification, a program definition by CII-Honeywell-Bull of France was agreed upon in 1979. The next task was to develop compilers for Ada and to evaluate them for effective and efficient use. It will obviously be some time before Ada becomes available to the general public.

[†] For once not an acronym but a recognition of the work of Blaise Pascal.
[††] Parallel processing is needed so as to be able to program functions with simultaneous activities.

2.3.2 The Essence of Programming

"What technological development will do is to reduce the need for a programmer to have any specific expertise in computing, so that creative individuals in many intellectual disciplines will be able to use computers directly to solve problems for themselves. . . . ." (Barron 1978).

It would be wrong to give the impression that programming is easy; it is a skill which takes time to acquire. The process of learning a high level language is very much akin to learning a foreign tongue but with the distinct advantage that computer languages have as few as twenty nouns, no adjectives, few verbs and very simple, if somewhat rigid, sentence structures.

The means of expressing operational instructions or algorithm solutions in a purposely defined code or language is not confined to computer programming. There are a number of far older illustrations to be found in our everyday activities, a prime example being the knitting pattern. A typical row of a simple pattern might be

K.4,P.4,*K.3,P.3,* rep to last 8 sts,K.4,P.4(76)

where K and P stand for the basic stitch types, knit and purl respectively. This program describes how to work this particular row; it consists of 76 stitches or knots, the first and last eight being 4 knits followed by 4 purls. The central part of the pattern is made up of a repeated section of 3 knits and 3 purls.

If we were to express this procedure in a high level Pascal-type language, it would be of the form:

```
begin
    knit(4);
    purl(4);
    stitchcount:= 8;
    while stitchcount < 76−8 do
    begin
        knit(3); purl(3);
        stitchcount:=stitchcount+6
    end;
    knit(4);
    purl(4)
end.
```

A knitting pattern is an excellent example of something that appears completely unintelligible to the uninitiated but which is perfectly obvious to one who knits i.e. uses the language. The same is true of computer programs; the example above is easily understood by anyone who has done even a little programming, whereas if it was completely new to you then, no doubt, it did not make much sense. People who are completely happy with knitting patterns must wonder why we have bothered to develop programming languages, when glorified knitting codes could have been used on all our computers! Music scores are a further example of a well known symbolic code.

One feature of a computer program, regardless of language, is that the instructions are 'obeyed', one at a time, in a well defined sequence. In this way they are similar to cooking recipes where operations occur in a specific order. Most recipes begin by defining all the ingredients required in the entire process. This sensible practice is also applied in many programming languages, such as ALGOL and Pascal where all the variables and commodities to be used are defined or declared at the head of the program. A Pascal program is divided into definition and execution sections. This distinction has been a great help to programmers in their quest for error free programs.

The only way to become proficient at programming is to practice. Just as a natural language can only be improved by speaking, a computer programmer must spend time writing test programs in order to improve his or her technique. Eventually one can conceptualise real problems in terms of the language just as knitting patterns became second nature to people familiar with them. Since most microcomputers now have the programming language BASIC on them, this is probably the best language to start with. Provisions to make programming courses more accessible, either as part of an adult education syllabus or government retraining scheme, will hopefully be improved in the future, although financial support will be needed. Until then, programming will remain a somewhat elitist activity, only available to those groups or individuals able to afford their own small computer.

There are many books available introducing the BASIC programming language to users with a small personal microcomputer. If you understand the algebraic equation

$$x = a + b$$

then you should have no difficulties programming in BASIC.

Unfortunately, one problem that does surround BASIC is that of dialects. Just as American English is different from the Australian variety, so one microcomputer's version of BASIC may well be slightly different from that of another machine. Generally, however, each microcomputer manufacturer provides a full description of the actual language used by their machine and forthcoming attempts to standardise on a single version of BASIC may help.

Once the user is sufficiently proficient in BASIC and the tasks required of the computer become more complex, involving longer and more tortuous programs, then it is advisable to explore the other languages for which the machine is suited. The first language is of course the most difficult to learn but, once this hurdle has been cleared, other types are merely variations or progressions from this and many books introducing other high level languages, such as Pascal, are readily available.

2.4 FROM ATOMIC BOMBS TO WAR GAMES

The previous sections have been concerned with the development of the modern microcomputer, from its stillbirth in the last century to the fertile product of today. Refinements in the basic design are evident both in the technology of the hardware and in the sophistication of the software. What is of more importance to the non-specialist, however, is the use of these machines and not their internal construction. It is perhaps misleading to consider the application of computers in a separate section divorced from their development, because the two areas are fundamentally linked. Most if not all of the improvements in computer technology have been initiated by user need, usually in the form of lower cost, smaller physical size, greater memory capability and speed.

The microprocessor was invented neither by accident nor as the result of purely abstract research; its development was the result of both market and military pressure. Similarly, the one million component chip will become a reality if, and only if, market research reveals that it would be profitable to produce. The same applies to software development; computer languages and programming aids exist primarily because manufactures need them in order to sell their machines. Although a considerable amount of research in language specification and formal problem solving has been the result of academic work, the major advancements have originated from commercial motivation. It takes a lot of time, effort and money to introduce a new computer system, especially if it makes use of advanced technologies; the market forces must be strong to warrant these changes.

To examine why computer equipment and facilities are what they are today, one must look at the applications that have influenced their progress. Once the social forces which have shaped today's technology are appreciated, the pressures society is making on future technology can be analysed.

"The urgent point of highlighting the social origins of microelectronics is to avoid the conclusion arrived at by so many commentators – that society is and will be determined by technology" (Webster 1980)

The work of Charles Babbage is a classic example of a development before its time; in 1830 there was neither the technology to realise his dreams nor the potential applications to justify the acquisition of such computing aids. The history of calculating machines continued along analogue lines leaving Babbage's digital concepts to lie dormant for a hundred years.

Four isolated areas formed the major impetus for the renaissance of the digital idea, namely:

1. Large scale government data processing. (US census collations).
2. Numerical solutions of difficult mathematical problems. (Ballistic calculations).
3. Atomic weapons research.
4. Solution of logical problems. (Cryptography).

2.4.1 Post World War Two Developments

The four application areas listed above, although not exhaustive, illustrate the social factors leading to the development of the first computers. Because of the high cost, large size and delicate nature of these early machines, it was not envisaged that they would have any universal use outside science; in fact, a report of the period declared that a handful of machines would satisfy, permanently, global requirements. What this report failed to realise was that computing technology was in its infancy and the previously narrow view taken of the scope of application would be shattered once reliable machines were available.

The first non-military groups to acquire computers were the universities and research institutes, government agencies and the big national and multinational companies. The expansion of universities throughout the sixties together with the emergence of subjects such as nuclear physics fostered the need for faster and faster computational devices and programming facilities. Languages such as FORTRAN were developed to enhance the *number crunching* abilities of the machines.

Commerce had somewhat different demands upon computers. The trend towards automated data processing predated the electronic computer, but once it became possible to use computers to manipulate data coded onto cards this trend gathered considerable pace. Pressure to replace the clumsy card records by more appropriate media soon followed; magnetic tapes, drums and discs found a ready market and this encouraged manufacturers to include larger and faster-operation backing (or secondary) storage with their computers. Banks, which were among the first commercial institutions to become heavily committed to computers, helped to pioneer the *remote access* mode of operation. Here, one or more large computers are used to hold all the available information in a *data base*; access to this data is then made possible from a number of different places, namely branch offices. In addition to the new hardware required to perform these operations, software was needed to enhance both efficient information retrieval and the overall security of the data base. Airlines were quick to realise the significance of this type of system and introduced it into their seat reservation procedures, so that travel agents all over the country could see what vacancies were available and book them automatically as required. A popular management trend in the 1960s was centralisation, and this was exactly what the computer facilitated. Although a large computing system was expensive, a period of monetary boom made a computer affordable as a status symbol even if not a strict economic necessity. It is interesting to note that just as the computer of the sixties matched the philosophy of the decade, the decentralised trend of the seventies has been accompanied by the evolution of the microcomputer, well tailored to a distributed approach to company strategy.

Throughout the late sixties and early seventies, improvements were being made in the hardware of the basic integrated circuit computer and yet there continued to be a large number of potential applications which were not economically feasible on the systems available. In an attempt to meet this demand, a number of manufacturers, DEC (Digital Equipment Corporation) in particular, produced much smaller and cheaper computers and by increasing reliability, running costs were also reduced. Because of these characteristics, the machines became known as minicomputers, their larger relations being called mainframes. One of the advantages of minicomputers, from the producer's viewpoint, was that these machines could adapt more easily to improvements in technology, such as the advent of microelectronic circuitry. However, before considering the chip and why it evolved when it did, attention should be given to one further area of application, which although slower to start has had a profound effect upon the development of modern computing.

Process Control
Computers have had a short but impressive history in the automatic control of industrial plant and processes; they have been used in situations where:

(a) Processes are complex or high-speed.
(b) Environment is hazardous to human safety.
(c) Quality control is important.
(d) Profit/output can be improved (crucial factor).
(e) Plant information needs preprocessing in order to be intelligible to the operators.

Two of the problems that faced early industrial computers were the hostile environment and the reliability expectations of the plant designers. The environment was improved by more efficient air-conditioning equipment but reliability, although steadily improving, has taken a lot longer to reach acceptable levels. Further difficulties arose in the interfacing of digital computers to continually operating industrial equipment.

Within the industrial setting, it soon became impossible for a single computer, no matter how large, to undertake all the operational functions that were now open to computer control in a typical process system. As well as the danger of having the entire plant under the direction of a single machine, the speed at which control loops needed to be handled for efficiency or safety was often beyond the scope of a single processor. It became essential to develop distributed systems consisting of a number of smaller machines each performing one task in the control process. The first minicomputer, the Westinghouse P50, was used for this purpose in 1964 at the Chocolate Bayon Biodegradable Detergent Plant. Since chemical plants are themselves distributed, it would appear apposite for the computer system to adopt similar characteristics; but there is then the problem of how to best transmit data and instructions between one computer and another. A whole theory of *computer networks* has evolved to consolidate these techniques, and technologies concerned with fibre-optics have been created to meet new requirements.

Indisputably, improvements in process control have both increased the efficiency of industrial processes and decreased the numbers and skills of many of the traditional jobs in such industries. To a large extent these effects were hidden during the sixties because of expansion in chemical production. Whether this will also happen with the microprocessor is far from clear. (see Chapter 3).

2.4.2 The Military and the Microprocessor

In both Britain and the US, computers were originally constructed for military purposes. Given this somewhat ominous beginning it is, perhaps, not surprising that many of the more recent innovations in computer design and operation have been initiated by the rigid requirements of the armed services for operational capabilities. Although commercial and industrial users have undoubtedly had some influence on the developing technology, no other factor has had so great an effect as the US military budget. Whilst Europe was rebuilding after the Second World War, the US had to contend with the Korean War and the equally taxing Cold War. Military thinking was focussed on the development of a nuclear "deterrent" and an effective defence system. A string of monitoring stations was set up across North America (and later in Europe) and computers had to be designed to collect and collate information provided by these installations. Space monitoring and strategic weapons guidance became an impossible task for humans. The next 'advance' was to move the computer from the defence base into the aircraft or tank, which necessitated small and robust computers, a development sponsored by the United States government. The final big push for the microcomputer was fuelled by the space race which in both the US and the USSR came under the auspices of the military. Power demands, weight, size and reliability were critical factors in the design of space capsules; in addition, sophisticated computer software and hardware were required by ground control. The computer manufacturers were fitting more and more components onto the integrated circuit board until in 1971 a complete microprocessor could be fitted on a single slab of silicon less than 0.25 sq cms in area.

Although the fervour of the original space race has subsided, military spending has not. The US armed forces buy more microprocessors than anyone else and modern weapons contain a level of automation that many commentators consider alarming. An up-to-date fighter plane such as the RAF's Tornado has, typically, five minicomputers on board as well as hundreds, if not thousands, of micros. In these planes, the pilot's actions are first "vetted" by the appropriate processor and during manoeuvres such as low-flying, evasive action can be taken by the plane without his knowledge (he would take too long). The technical difficulties presented by such systems are immense but they do represent intriguing and compelling problems to many computer scientists. To tackle some of these difficulties, the high level language Ada is being designed and produced by the efforts of many groups, both in Europe and the US. Eventually, Ada will become widely available and its general purpose nature will render it applicable to all manner of problems; its existence, however, will be due solely to the many millions of dollars spent on the project during its formative stages. This money has come entirely from the US Department of Defense budget. Another, now well used, language which owes its existence to the same source is COBOL:

> "The Department of Defense was pleased to undertake this project; in fact, we were embarrassed that the idea for such a common language had not had its origin by that time in Defense since we would benefit so greatly from the success of such a project. . . ." (Phillips 1978)

A different area of computing in which the Pentagon has also been particularly interested is war games; it is said that during the Vietnam war, many of the airborn attacks were first played out on a large mainframe computer. Today, complicated computer games are run by the Pentagon which both test the nation's defences and update their strategies or tactics. Christopher Evans considers that, with computers now in control of decision making in both the Russian and American defence organisations, international conflict between superpowers could not occur; computers would never sanction a policy which would result in extensive loss of life. (Evans 1979b). Unfortunately, the timing of the television presentation of Evan's book in 1979 led to such assertions being broadcast only four days after the United States military had, for over six minutes, thought that it was under nuclear attack. One of the computer game tapes, which simulated an enemy missile salvo, had been loaded by mistake and was presumed to be genuine. Human error may eventually be blamed for the incident, but a system open to such errors is hardly secure and engenders no confidence. Another explanation, of course, could be that it was just an exercise. In which case the Pentagon must be alarmed by the number of defence personnel who ignored the computer messages and assumed that the system was malfunctioning again!

To return to 1971, the micro emerged from its exclusively military context when Intel released it's 4-bit microprocessor. Sales of microelectronic products such as calculators and digital watches soon encouraged other companies of which Texas Instruments and Motorola were among the most successful, into the field. The 4-bit micro was soon superseded by the more useful, now standard 8-bit variety, and the small memory incorporated into the processor chip was soon inadequate for many potential applications. In response to demand it has become normal to expect the microelectronics industry to double the complexity of its products every two years!

In 1975 Fairchild ploughed back 12% of income into research, with Intel and Data General not far below this level. Even IBM's 6.6% represents over £1 billion. The fruits of this expenditure are seen in the increased complexity of their products. Fig. 2.4 shows the rise in the number of components per chip and the price per component over the years 1965-80. Although the cost of research is increasing and the possibility of one's competitors copying innovatory designs more real, there is no immediate reason why this graph should not continue in its present direction for the foreseeable future.

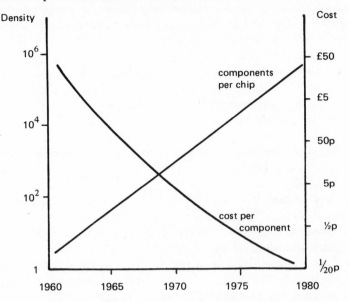

Fig. 2.4 – The year by year increase in the complexity of the chip, and decrease in the cost per component.

What are microprocessors used for? The two largest consumers are the military and the computer industry. But the largest manufacturer of micros, IBM, uses its entire supply within its other products; they are not sold on the open market. So where, outside the two vast areas, does the "all pervasive" micro find employment? In 1979 a Department of Industry publication (Simmons 1979) divided applications into five general categories:

1. *Enhancement of existing products:* including vehicles, lift controls, cash registers, washing machines, cameras etc.
2. *New products:* word-processors, miniature television sets, electric pianos, personal computers, computer games etc.
3. *Industrial and other control systems:* continuous process equipment, electrical goods, materials handling, transport, medical engineering, agriculture etc.
4. *Data processing:* order processing, banking transactions, production scheduling, library control etc.
5. *New techniques and equipment in Communications:* data communication equipment, viewdata, electronic typesetting, point-of-sale terminals, System X telephone exchange, electronic funds transfer etc.

This is by no means a comprehensive list; in fact, it is probably more difficult to think of products that CANNOT have a micro attached!

The most straightforward applications are those in which the microprocessor is embedded into other equipment, such as an automatic washing machine or a car's ignition system. The micro's job is simply to control the equipment by continually executing a set of instructions, permanently stored in its ROM (Read Only Memory). This type of microprocessor cannot truly be called a complete system because the instructions are fixed and nobody can alter the operational cycle of the device. Nevertheless, there are a number of benefits that, for example, a washing machine manufacturer could obtain by incorporating microelectronics into their wares:

(i) *Simplicity;* building control logic in conventional technology is very complicated.

(ii) *Reliability* of equipment.

(iii) *Material savings:* a micro is at least a thousand times smaller than previous circuitry.

(iv) *Labour savings:* it takes fewer and less skilled workers to assemble micro embedded products.

(v) *Repair savings:* because of (ii) and the modular structure of the equipment. If a fault occurs, the entire micro can be exchanged for a new one, so that repairing is also 'deskilled'.

(vi) *Increased facilities:* the micro does not just replace the old logic, it opens up extra possibilities.

For other manufacturers, such as camera makers, old style logic would not fit into the products, therefore (iii) can have a dual benefit.

New products, including those in the fields of data processing and communication, will arrive when they become economically feasible. Before discussing in the next chapter ways of assessing these microelectronic applications, one should consider in detail two important areas of microprocessor development. These are *information technology* and *robotics,* which, between them, represent the greatest threat and the most positive challenge to our social and economic order.

2.4.3 Information Technology

Prophets of the post-industrial society predict that the major commodity of the future will not be electricity, nor power, but information. Moreover, they assert that the manipulation and dissemination of this information will become a crucial sector in the economy, employing most of the working population. The case for an information 'explosion' is so far unproven although there has been a data explosion in recent years. The initial culprit was the photocopier, which made it possible to give everyone in any organisation a copy of any document.

There is no evidence, however, that this leads to better informed people. Similarly, an expensive computer system enables a company to store in its data bases unlimited quantities of trivial and insignificant data. This alone does not provide management with any greater depth of information than before. Obviously, as societies become more interwoven and interdependent even across national frontiers, the amount of useful information which will need to flow between physically separate places will grow. Whether this increase will constitute an explosion remains to be seen, but what cannot be denied is the need for data processing and communications systems.

Office Equipment
A typical commercial office will probably have obtained a typewriter around the turn of the century, an electronically assisted replacement during the 1960's and a photocopier ten years later. In the same period, the volume of work passing through such an office would have increased tremendously. Whereas the automation of data processing activities within the larger organisations has had a relatively long history, it has hitherto been uneconomic to introduce computer-aided equipment into the ordinary office. This picture has changed, and micro-computer systems are now being used to perform a variety of clerical tasks.

As commerce has become more standardised, so have the documents issuing from our typical office. To meet this trend the *word-processor* has been developed to facilitate, amongst other things, the automatic production of standard letters and contracts etc. A word-processor consists of a typewriter style keyboard and, a television type screen or other form of display which shows what has been typed. When a copy is required of some previously checked and corrected document, it is run off on a special high-quality fast printer; files are magnetic copies on a form of backing storage, such as floppy discs. Essentially, the word-processor is an ordinary microcomputer, with specialised software allowing alterations and additions to previously typed text; this can then be printed in the desired format, for example with visually pleasing right and left justified margins. Because of this software, a complete word-processor system is still considerably more expensive than the actual hardware would warrant, even though a single costly printer can be shared between all the work units. As sales of software escalate, word processing equipment should fall in price and come within the reach of many more organisations; in fact, many of the personal computer companies already offer word processing packages for their machines at a comparatively low cost.

Although general speculations on future developments have been resisted in this book, one type of equipment that will inevitably become available — thanks to massive research and development expenditure — is the voice recognition input device, by which verbal directions are transformed into print. This could well have a devastating effect upon secretarial work, but only if management chooses to produce their own letters and other documents by such methods.

Historical evidence indicates that this is far from being the normal reaction. Managers have preferred in the past to keep themselves at least one step removed from ultra modern aids.

Although the microprocessor will bring a number of gadgets to the office, such as electronic diaries and automated filing systems, it is the word-processor which is fundamentally changing the traditional office structure. As with so many applications of 'new technology' its origin was seeded in a pre-computer, let alone a pre-micro, era. The need to correct speedily the inevitable mistakes made while typing led, in the late thirties and forties, to the design of typewriters that had a small memory attached. A later popular model, the IBM Selectric machine, incorporated a magnetic tape from which previously typed documents could be recalled for correction. Paper tape machines have also made use of this method. It is no surprise, therefore, that the microcomputer has found such a ready market with this sort of device; it has not forced itself into the office but has been pulled by an application area waiting for the necessary cheap processing power to evolve.

Telecommunications

The individual word-processor unit will become an increasingly useful and progressively more available tool to office workers and writers in general. The nature of information is however, that once created it needs to be communicated elsewhere. The oldest organised postal service began in London early in the 17th century; by 1812, the service had spread over the nation but the price had become prohibitive. A letter from London to Edinburgh, for example, would have cost 1s 1d [about 6p, although worth about £1 today]. This situation was changed by Rowland Hill's report on 'Postal Reform' in 1837. He advocated, amongst other things, a single 1d prepaid charge for all letters irrespective of their destination. The implementation of these ideas in 1839 led to the first real public postal service. Even before the postal service there have been occasions when it has proved necessary to send signals quickly across the nation. Probably the oldest technique was lighting beacons on the hill tops; other forms of signalling were bells, flags and semaphores. With the harnessing of electricity these were all superseded by the telegraph system, which became widespread in the middle of the 19th century. By 1925, these systems had improved to such a point that a normal keyboard had been incorporated and the messages themselves were punched onto paper tape to be transcribed by coding apparatus — a method later employed on computers.

The most far-reaching development in communications has been the telephone, now the most common mode of disseminating information. The obvious drawback of the ordinary telephone system was that only verbal messages could be transmitted. For an organisation which stores data electronically (magnetically) or creates documents on a word-processor, there is considerable advantage if such information can be transmitted along the telephone wires. Rather than printing the message onto a piece of paper that has then to be posted in the traditional fashion, many companies, especially in the United States, transmit the data digitally over the telephone, a process known as *electronic mail.* The advantages of speed and paper conservation are easily recognised, particularly if the information can be handled electronically at its destination.

One of the first computer network systems to incorporate an electronic mail facility was ARPANET (Advanced Research Projects Agencies NETwork) which links research establishments and universities in the US and Europe, and was developed by the US Department of Defense. Mailbox facilities are now available on many computer networks and information systems. They have become the most straightforward way of keeping in touch with co-workers and colleagues in many different locations. Furthermore, not only can letters and messages be transmitted electronically; with the right equipment, complicated forms, diagrams and pictures can be broken down, sent across the world and then recreated in a matter of minutes. This technique is known as 'facsimile transmission', a crude yet effective example of which was demonstrated as early as 1878.

To establish a national telecommunications system in the UK requires specialist equipment and a large budget. As a result research has mainly been carried out by the Post Office (now British Telecom). As well as launching their own viewdata service they have developed a new telephone exchange called System X, a digital, computer controlled switching and transmission system which is to replace conventional exchanges and the Telex service. System X is quicker than the conventional exchange and less prone to failure; when it does fail, calls will automatically be re-routed around the offending equipment. It also has its own voice synthesiser and is designed for unattended operation. Because it is digital, word-processors and other computer equipment can be connected to the system without the need for expensive slow modems.[†] Other 'benefits' of the system can be measured in terms of natural wastage and voluntary redundancies, both within British Telecom and the Post Office.

The British Government decision, in 1980, to split the Post Office into telecommunication and letter handling sections illustrates the direct competition that will soon develop between electronic and conventional mail. The electronic system is automatic and quick while the conventional system is slow, often unreliable and requires personnel to work a 6 day, 42 hour week often at unsocial hours. To participate in the traditional method, however, requires only a letter-box in the front door whilst electronic mail needs a telephone line and a substantial piece of computer hardware. As more and more businesses go over to the fast system, the conventional one will become increasingly uneconomic and hence more expensive. Previously the structure of the Post Office enabled the telecom-

---

[†] A MOdulator/DEModulator is a digital/analogue converter which allows digital signals to be sent along conventional analogue telephone lines.

muncations sector to subsidise letter handling; unless postage rates continue to be protected from market forces, the cost of sending a letter may rise substantially.

International communications will be achieved by the use of satellites, a number of which are already in operation, such as the Franco-German *Symphonie* which links IBM computer systems. Large capital investment is needed to launch a satellite programme but it is, perhaps, some indication of the envisaged growth of international data processing that so many of the larger computer groups are planning to offer a comprehensive satellite service. Experiments on Symphonie have taken the form of a link between four points, two in the USA, one in Germany and one in France. So far, data exchange rates to the order of 1.544 million binary digits per second have been achieved (COMSAT 1979).

2.4.4 Robotics
There is nothing new about the concept of automation or robotics. Ever since the first industrial revolution there has been a continuous movement away from direct involvement in the manufacturing process. The harnessing of steam and electricity removed the worker's burden of providing the motive power for production. This was followed by gradual improvements in the sophistication of tools of the trade, with the result that factory workers increasingly adopted the role of 'controller' over mechanised equipment.

As far back as 1805 Jacquard had introduced automated control into the industrial process; productivity and profit margins ensured the continuation of this trend, and with the availability of minicomputers a high level of automation was attained in industry. An early example of this was the rolling mills in the steel industry, where red-hot billets were passed through a series of computer controlled rollers to squash the steel into the desired shape. Once the required diameter was reached the rod was measured by sensors and this information relayed from the local minicomputer to a controlling computer which, with the help of a reasonably straightforward algorithm, calculated the best way of cutting the steel rod with least wastage. Before the use of computers the steel would have been cut into standard lengths, producing greater waste and a less flexible product range. The role of the worker in this system was of 'operator'. He or she no longer had control over the minute by minute activities but was more concerned with operating decisions – what action to take in this or that situation. Although fewer workers were needed on the shop floor, the overall knowledge required and the responsibility inherent in being an operator meant that the job was still highly skilled. Other production jobs, such as lathe work, have similarly been upgraded from a manual to a machine-controlled task, but for the generation of computers available in the sixties some industries, for instance production-line car assembly, proved too complicated for such simulation.

The microcomputer has made potentially economic robots available. Robots have sufficient computer power to make decisions and to deal with the complicated task or unforeseen circumstance. In the rolling mill example, if a rod was bent or broken the human operator would assume control and deal with the situation. Although the process was automated, the computer was not capable of operating under strange conditions and so the worker had to retain the skills of the manual system and use them when necessary. On the other hand, because of the flexibility of its design and the level of incorporated hardware and software a robot can 'learn' from its environment. It can copy a human worker and hence be used to assemble cars or pack chocolates; moreover, a 'seeing' robot can recognise components so that it will not weld a wing mirror to the windscreen of the car.

In short, the robot can assume the role of operator, leaving the worker downgraded to 'supervisor' (robot minder). If the process goes wrong or some machinery breaks down, the supervisor will be instructed as to what action to take and who to inform. The work is easier, but the psychological effects of such a job could be far from good. Another area in which complete automation is being attempted is mining. The National Coal Board have already invested over 10 million pounds in Minos (MINe Operating System) with twenty-four pits equipped. As well as the manpower implications, considerable concern has been expressed as to how this equipment will be used, what information will be monitored, who will control it and how the traditional job grading system will be implemented alongside Minos (Feickert 1979). These problems are by no means confined to the mining industry and will be discussed in more detail in Chapter 3.

Some of the first jobs to which robots were applied included paint spraying and welding, and in the future they will find particular application in unpleasant or dangerous environments (the nuclear power industry will probably employ many robots). Because of low investment levels we have been slow to exploit robots in the UK; whether this will prove an economic disaster or a social benefit remains to be seen.

It is hoped that the above examples illustrate that microelectronics opens up not one but many possible futures. Technology has gone in the direction it was pushed hardest and social pressures have decided where it was and was not applied and to what extent it proved to be beneficial or otherwise. To try to extrapolate this analysis into the future requires an assessment of the technology available and of the areas whose needs will furnish its applications.

In considering the evolution of the micro there are a number of implementations and uses which have not been mentioned but which, in their own small way, have influenced the progression from ENIAC to the Z80. Meteorology, the production of handicap aids and traffic control are but three; other applications, such as education and small firms, will be discussed later. If one ever needed to be reminded of the power of the microprocessor over its ancestors, then remember, the next time you play (or swear at!) 'Space Invaders' that the game is more sophisticated than the machine on which the first atomic bomb was designed.

3

Assessing Microelectronic Technology

From even the short historical account laid out in the previous chapter it should be clear that the microprocessor, as with other forms of computing, has effects and influences that extend beyond their immediate surrounds and specific functions. This is not only the position with microelectronics; in our heavily interdependent society any significant technological change will bring with it a host of economical and environmental consequences, many of which will appear at least initially, to be unpredictable. It is reasonable to expect that the micro which represents such a dramatic technical change will precipitate debate and argument on such far ranging topics as unemployment, privacy, education, social order and information systems. Yet to discuss such diverse subjects in isolation with no reference back to the technology itself, as many commentators have done, would obscure an overall view of microelectronics. This view will be central to the development of criteria as to what are appropriate and inappropriate methods of designing and using micro-based technologies. How is it possible then to assess microelectronics 'per se'? Four general questions that might be asked about any technology are:

1. How does it work?
2. What techniques are required in manufacture?
3. How is it used and by whom?
4. How will it affect people and systems not directly concerned with its use?

The categories are of course not independent; how it works relies to some extent on how it is manufactured, which in turn depends on the ultimate use. All of these three then influence the overall effects. Although these four questions outline the general areas of concern, they need to be made more specific for actual analysis. Detailed questions might take the form:

1. *How Does it Work?*
   (a) What level of education and training is required to fully understand the technology?
   (b) To what conceptual level can the technology be understood by the user and the public?
   (c) Are the necessary technical data readily and easily available?
   (d) What are the inherent properties of the technology?

2. *What Technologies are Required in Manufacture?*
   (a) What are the social, economic and environmental costs of production?
   (b) What skills are required by the work force?
   (c) How reliable and safe is the manufacturing process?

3. *How is it Used and by Whom?*
   (a) What are the environmental and economic costs of its use?
   (b) What objectives does its use serve?
   (c) How successful is it in fulfilling these objectives?
   (d) Who decides upon and controls its application?
   (e) What skills are required by its users?
   (f) What are the psychological benefits and problems associated with its application?

4. *How Will it Effect Non-Users?*
   (a) What does it cost the community as a whole?
   (b) Who gains from its use and who loses?
   (c) How does the new technology interact with society?
   (d) What would be the social, environmental and economic disturbances?

Many of these questions have already been highlighted in Chapter 2 and it is worthwhile reconsidering the history of computers, bearing them in mind. Other points, in particular those dealing with environmental and psychological factors will be taken up later; the present chapter focusses attention upon the wider social implications of microelectronics. It is this area that has rightly been at the forefront of public concern over the New Technology.

3.1 SCALE AND EFFICIENCY

Before embarking on a discussion of actual problem areas we must return to ·question 1(d) — namely, what are the inherent properties of the technology? By pin-pointing these factors we can compare widely differing applications and obtain criteria by which secondary effects may well be predicted and a more appropriate method of using micros established.

Microprocessors as with other microelectronic components are minute relatively cheap and very reliable. Microcomputers themselves, although they consist of a keyboard, secondary storage and a VDU screen in addition to these chips, are still comparatively inexpensive and, with a little inconvenience, portable. When compared to old style logic and large computers it is clear that microelectronics is not just an improved version of former technology, and with its operational parameters so different from that of its predecessors it truly deserves the title 'New Technology'. In all measurements such as cost, reliability, size, power requirement and flexibility, it is far removed from anything previously produced or even envisaged. Certainly there are areas where the micro can still learn from its larger brother — provision of high-level languages for example — but these factors are easily outweighed by the advantages of micros. Given these fundamental properties it is reasonable to assume that the introduction of microelectronic devices will not pass unnoticed in whatever economic, manufacturing, data processing or information gathering system they appear. Even if the micro is only being used in a specific area, the ramifications may well spread throughout the entire system. A shift in the natural scale of only one part of an operation may well transform a system that was previously well-balanced into one that has a number of undesirable features. It is from a lack of appreciation of the scope of changes that many of the unfortunate consequences of the Mighty Micro appear.

In order to predict the possible effects of introducing microelectronic equipment into certain processes we must isolate the properties of the system most likely to alter due to changes in scale. Two immediate candidates for consideration are the existence of constraints and the criteria for measuring efficiency. Most systems, be they entire economies, management organisation, newspaper production or mail deliveries, operate within what have become natural and often unrealised constraints. Computerisation can instantly destroy these constraints and, unless planning and redesign starts again from square one, the result will be unpredictable and possibly undesirable. Computer aided teaching is an entirely different process from that which uses chalk and board; the automatic referencing of personal medical records bears no resemblance to the manual system despite the fact that the data pertaining to any individual may well be identical; as described in the previous chapter, electronic mail operates under totally different constraints to the conventional method.

A new area of potential conflict stems from too narrow a definition of the term 'efficiency'. What has been taken in the past as a reasonable measure of overall performance may be far from adequate with a new system. Computers are efficient; microprocessor equipment can be very efficient but this does not imply its effective use. A micro can process information in billionths of a second but its introduction to a company, office or industry does not guarantee an economic gain. Even where it can be shown to be a local success financially, there is still the wider socio-economic balance to consider. A profitable action to one firm may be a financial burden to the state or a loss of job satisfaction to their work force.

Dissatisfaction with all types of innovatory technologies is more pronounced where their adoption have been forced upon employees. The decision as to whether and how to introduce microcomputer equipment is invariably taken 'at the top', even though the cost of such systems is low enough not to warrant this. As a result, the decision to purchase the computer system is often made without the participation of the people who will have to use it — they have to fit in as best they can when the equipment arrives. Only recently has there been any detailed attempt to specify and develop appropriate man-machine interfaces. One group, although their work is still incomplete, have illustrated what is really only common sense — that any computer system is only as efficient as its human link.†

Another related theme that prevails in the application of the New Technology is the degree to which a user must change his or her work patterns in order to obtain the best of the new equipment. Sales personnel rarely realise the transition they make when they move from talking about computer aids, to systems which force the user to change role. The microcomputer is the new efficient device therefore *WE* must change in order to make the most of it. It would be difficult to find an example of a computer which is running inefficiently with the express purpose of giving the operator a more interesting or responsible job. Changes in work practices are desirable if they are to our overall benefit but not if they are merely sacrifices to computer efficiency.

The remaining sections of this chapter deal with some of the most pressing areas of potential disharmony that have arisen or are liable to arise as a result of microelectronics. Whilst assessing the problems one should bear in mind the questions posed at the beginning of this chapter and consider to what extent conflicts have developed because natural constraints have been superseded and traditional measures of efficiency have become socially or economically, outdated.

3.2 UNEMPLOYMENT

The social implications of microelectronics focus sharply upon the issue of unemployment, a problem which, it is argued, could well be compounded by advances in microtechnology. Given that a person's job or trade is still, in many industrial nations, the single most important social label, it is not surprising that unemployment brings with it not only financial hardship but also deep psychological problems. Since employment plays such a central role within society it is understandable that a substantial threat to a persons status will be met with much specualtion, conjecture, and conflict.

> "History shows that each time there has been a significant increase in productivity, this has been followed by unemployment and a severe depression . . . It is facile to expect that the technology will create jobs faster than it destroys them."
> I. M. Barron (1978) — INMOS

† Medical Research Council, Applied Psychology Unit, Cambridge; in conjunction with IBM UK Laboratories Ltd., Winchester.

"There is a choice. Remain as we are, reject the new technology and we face unemployment of up to 5.5 million by the end of the century. Embrace the new technology, accept the challenge and we end up with unemployment of about 5 million." Clive Jenkins and Barrie Sherman (1979) – ASTMS

"The general conclusion which emerges from the analysis, with exceptions in particular areas, is that over the next five to ten years the effects of micro-electronic technology in reducing industries demands for labour are unlikely to be any more dramatic than those of many previous examples of technological improvement." J. Sleigh et al – Report by the Department of Employment (1979).

These are just a small selection of the many statements that have been made about the future of work in the UK. Microelectronics is attacking employment levels both by accelerating the trend towards automation and by forcing radical re-designs of many traditional products, and yet the micro is far from being the only cause of potential job loss. In the UK the official unemployment level has been over one million since the mid seventies and passed the two million level in 1980; the actual figure including those who do not register is even higher. In addition, it is estimated that to maintain the same percentage of people employed an extra two and a half million jobs will be required by 1991, due to an expansion of the population in Britain. Although the national unemployment figure is an influential statistic both economically and politically, it inevitably conceals many other features of the workings of the economy. Arguments as to whether the micro will cause four, five or zero million unemployed can, if taken no further, be very misleading. Regional trends, female employment and the future of semi-skilled work are just three of the 'secondary' effects which will undoubtedly be of more immediate importance to many members of the community. The following section on *Tomorrow's Jobs* will deal with these aspects.

One of the first reports on the possible social and economic implications of microelectronics implications of microelectronics was produced by Simon Nora (1978) for the French government in 1977-78. This report estimated that within the medium term (approximately ten years) telematiques[†] would cause banks and insurance companies to reduce their staff by over thirty per cent. Social Security and Post Office workers would suffer similar reductions but over a longer time-scale. Office and industrial staff would also be affected. Since the Nora Report there have been a number of influential and prestigious organisations predicting a variety of possible and probable future trends; these include the Cambridge Economic Policy Group, the Science Policy Research Unit of the University of Sussex (SPRU) and the Advisory Council for Applied Research and Development.

All analyses hinge on attempts to quantify the following two effects:

1. Displacement of traditional jobs.
2. Creation of new jobs.

[†] The combination of telecommunications and data processing.

Both these categories incorporate the dual problems of estimating not only the final magnitude of these effects but also the rate at which they will take place.

Displacement of Traditional Jobs
Of the two, this is by far the easiest effect to analyse as it concerns jobs which already exist. Jenkins and Sherman considered over fifty industries and professions in the UK and obtained estimates of changes in a sample labour force, over the short, medium and long term. In the near future, lack of innovation and low investment will hold back the introduction of new techniques, (this was also found by Sleigh *et al*), but by 1993 they calculate that the reduction of jobs will be over 5,200,000 or 23.2%. These projections, though admitted by the authors to be 'hardly precise', are in rough agreement with both the NORA and SPRU reports. A similar, perhaps less severe, estimate has been made by the West German Ministry of Research and Technology with regard to their economy. (*Electronics and Jobs,* Bonn 1979).

Creation of New Jobs
Attempts to estimate the number of completely new jobs which should emerge as a result of microelectronic expansion is far more difficult. Some totally new products, such as pocket calculators, will bring with them a considerable number of jobs. Updated versions of older products, for instance the digital watch, create some employment at the expense of job loss elsewhere. Computer aided manufacturer and computer aided design will similarly produce job loss for certain types of work whilst opening up new employment in other areas. In addition, modern manufacturing equipment needs to be produced which, when installed, may lead to the acquisition of a greater share of international trade, thereby creating more jobs in Britain presumably at the expense of workers overseas. Another key factor in the discussion is the extent to which industry will adopt automated techniques in order to compete in expanding markets. The commitment to technological advances such as robots will result in less new employment than might have been expected had conventional methods been used.

If the manufacturing scene is a difficult one to evaluate, the service industries must be virtually impossible. Tom Stonier (1979) considers that by the end of this century only ten per cent of the workforce of any industrial nation will be involved in manufacture or agriculture – the rest will be either unemployed or at work in the service sector. Information systems such as Prestel could, within thirty years, employ directly and indirectly over one million people, whereas five years ago they employed vitually none. The rate at which this and other communication and service industries expand depends upon a number of international and largely unpredictable factors of which the availability of appropriate technology is but one; the price of oil and bank interest rate are both far more important indicators of future trends.

3.2.1 Three Possible Scenarios for the Future

Future levels of employment can only be measured effectively by quantitively comparing both the displacement and creation of jobs. This will result in a number of possible hypotheses, the accuracies of which will depend largely upon the rate at which jobs are found or lost. The two most straightforward predictions stem from the assumption that one rate will be continually greater than the other (Fig. 3.1) giving a permanent position of either overall surplus or shortage. A third possible prediction comes from a more complicated approach in which it is assumed that initially job creation will lag behind displacement, but that at some future point this situation will be reversed.

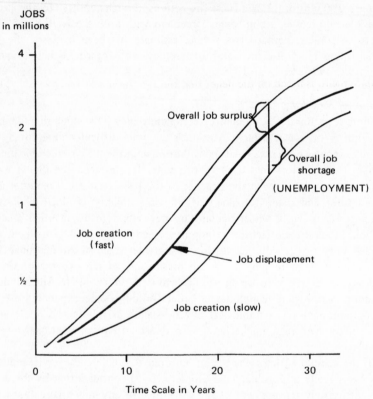

Fig. 3.1 – Job creation and displacement – permanently out of step.

Displacement Lags Behind Creation

This optimistic hypothesis as to the levels of future employment is also, unfortunately, the least supported. It originates from the assumption that there is nothing particularly special about microelectronics and that where it does cause changes they will occur slowly. Jobs will therefore not be lost at a significant rate and others should easily be created in the new industries. Although the traditional conservative nature of the UK management sector would uphold this view, innovatory uptake would have to be gradual, not only in Britain but worldwide. If a number of countries were substantially quicker in using the new technology their increased share of world trade through higher productivity would inevitably lead to recession and unemployment in other nations. Though no economist has seriously considered it plausible for job creation to overshadow loss there are a number of commentators who feel that these effects will be of a similar order. The Department of Employment, judging by the quote at the beginning of this section, feels that it is unlikely that job displacement will become seriously out of step with job creation.

Creation Lagging Permanently Behind Displacement
This second and most pessimistic view, implying permanent and increasing unemployment, is based on the belief that the very nature of the new technology involves structural job loss. Microelectronic tools are so economic and widely applicable that they can undertake a vast number of tasks currently available to workers. Moreover it is feared that the newly created industries will inevitably be highly automated and hence employ a minimal workforce. Jenkins and Sherman consider it unavoidable that unemployment levels of five and a half million will be witnessed in the UK by the end of this century. This will be incurred either by resisting modernisation which will also mean losing world trade, or by accomodating the new technology and widening the gap between displacement and creation.

It should be remembered here that the concept of employment and hence unemployment is not rigid. At the beginning of the industrial revolution the average working week was eighty hours, today it is less than forty and it seems reasonable to assume that this level will be decreased still further. In both the predictions outlined above it is assumed that there will be no major change in the structure of employment, nor in the central role it commands in society, before the year 2000. Were it possible in the short term to radically alter peoples views and social norms about the concept of work, then the rapid permanent dislocation of jobs could be seen as an acceleration towards the acquistion of leisure.

Short Term Job Loss − Long Term Gain
Engineers are familiar with systems that, when subjected to a step increase in one of the operating parameters, behave initially by exhibiting delayed or misleading reactions but which, in the long term, display a pronounced significant trend. Such a system is said to be lagged or to contain *dead time*. Microelectronics, if it does cause a quantum jump in productivity, can be interpreted as causing a step increase in one of the economy's predominant factors. As we witnessed when OPEC quadrupled oil prices in 1968, our financial system does not respond kindly to such rapid changes.

When we examine the history of industrialisation we can recognise a number of long term trends, one of which appears to be a 70 to 100 year cycle which starts with a major increase in productivity, is followed by economic depression and unemployment, but finishes with overall gains in social prosperity and work levels. This cyclic behaviour, which is similar in nature to Kondratieff's theory of long term economic waves, has in the past been initiated by the introduction of the steam engine, the electric motor and the railway network. Microelectronics, because of the pervasive way it can affect all aspects of modern industry, is a prime candidate as the instigator of a further cycle.

In case this prediction is accurate a number of crucial questions need to be asked. Fig. 3.2 illustrates the behaviour in terms of unemployment trends that could be expected from this model. But if analysis of the future is to be of any value, attempts must be made to quantify the predictions, in particular the length of time it would take to arrive at the breakthrough point, and to consider the interim maximum level of unemployment. Socially there can never

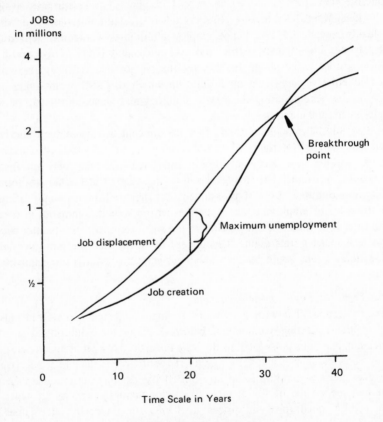

Fig. 3.2 – The third scenario.

be any acceptable level of unemployment, but even economically there is a point where it becomes impossible for the working population to support the unemployed. In this situation, any attempt to predict future trends is futile. Even before this level is reached, economic growth will be severely restricted and the break-through point postponed by high unemployment; as has often been said — "Robots can make but they cannot buy!"

3.2.2 Preventative Action
Analysis of future trends in employment, although of interest, is a pointless exercise unless it can indicate how such trends might be manipulated. But just as there are a number of theories concerning the likely effects of microelectronics, there are a variety of different responses advocated. These views tend to reflect not only which scenario is being supported but also, to a large extent, the economic and political philosphy of the observer.

Laissez Faire
This is the easiest option to implement since it involves taking no action at all! The belief here is that market forces will deal with any threat to employment and that these forces work best when they are not interfered with by government action. Supporters of this policy generally believe that there is nothing particularly special about microelectronics. Their assessment of the technology follows the lines of the first prediction in that it will not greatly affect social order and that any loss of traditional work will quickly be matched by the emergence of new jobs. The Cambridge Economic Policy Group have considered the likely implications of a 'do nothing' attitude by using the conventional Keynesian model with normal parameters. They used as their basic doctrine the assumption that government policies will not alter and that successive administrations will pursue, to a greater or lesser degree, tight fiscal controls and wage restraints in order to fight inflation. The Cambridge School predict that the resulting slow economic growth will result in 3 million unemployed by 1985 and 4.5 million by 1990. Such models are, of course, always open to misinterpretation and at best give results which are only approximate. Nevertheless, this analysis does give an indication of the likely consequences of a laissez faire attitude. Whether a government could continue to ignore unemployment when it reaches two and a half or three million is doubtful. Social unrest and fascism are historically associated with such levels and one can hope that a government would quickly reconsider its passive approach at the first sign of such consequences.

The Luddite Response
If, when assessing the effects of the new technology, you come to the conclusion that none of the benefits are coming in your direction then it is reasonable to react by simply opposing its introduction. Furthermore, if some labour-saving or skill-replacing device is forced onto the shop floor without prior negotiations or agreement it is understandable that workers either refuse to use it, use it ineffici-

ently or as an extreme measure, sabotage it. This response, which is by no means confined to microelectronics, is usually given the name 'Ludditism' after the Nottingham and West Yorkshire workers who, in 1812, countered the threat to croppers and stocking makers jobs by destroying new machinery and factories (Thomas 1970). A later and slightly more successful campaign was organised by 'Captain Swing' in South East England, when threshing machines were introduced in the local farms. After riots and rick burning, Norfolk magistrates recommended that owners and occupiers of land discontinue their use of threshers and increase wages (Hobsbawn 1969). Nedd Ludd and Captain Swing were both pseudonyms used to sign letters from the workers and they are now part of Trade Union folk lore.

Although in retrospect, both the thrasher and textile mechanisation have turned out to be of social benefit to the community at large, this would have been small comfort to the people who, at that time, were subject to the most deplorable living conditions because they could not find work. It is to be hoped that such widespread deprivation is no longer possible in this country and yet there remains the problem of how, as a community, we deal with the possibility of large, albeit possibly short-term, unemployment amongst particular groups of workers in certain geographical locations.

The main difficulty with the Luddite approach is that it cannot be co-ordinated world wide. Were it possible to obtain a universal agreement to unilaterally curtail the introduction of technology then no country would suffer exclusively. If one nation, however, took a solitary decision to oppose innovation the resulting low productivity, compared to that of other competing industrial countries, would result in high unemployment.

> "Is it better, one asks, to run a society in a deliberately inefficient way to provide work for all or is it better to have an efficient society, down-grading the importance of work and distributing the profits from that work more equitably?" (Jenkins 1979).

Other aspects of the micro have also contributed to the Luddite response. Fears that improvements in information handling will move society alarmingly close to a 'Big Brother' state of affairs have led a number of groups to the conclusion that only positive action will arrest this undesirable trend. This has taken the form of 'sensitive' magnetic tapes being mysteriously wiped clean, on the one hand, to the more extreme action that has taken place in Toulouse, where, at Philips Data Systems, over £200 000 worth of damage was caused by arson in April 1980, while at the same time, petrol bombs were used to destroy hardware at CII-Honeywell Bull. Other means of restricting personal-data handling will be discussed later in this chapter.

The Social Policy Response[†]

If high levels of unemployment are inevitable, either permanently or at best for

[†] This term was used by Tom Stonier (1979b)

a generation, then action must be taken now to ward off its worst consequences. The question of who controls technology and who benefits from its use must be faced by the trade unions, employers and government. A technology which makes work more rewarding, safer and cleaner whilst giving greater remuneration for less hours of activity is unlikely to provoke a Luddite reaction, but to get even some way toward these goals would require action and finance presently unforthcoming.

There are a number of measures which would collectively begin to constitute a social or appropriate response; firstly there should be a heavy reduction in the amount of time we all spend at work. This can be achieved by shortening the working week, taking longer holidays and much earlier retirement for those who wish it. Already many trade unions are calling for a 35 hour week and there is no reason why this should not be subsequently reduced to a 30, 25 or even 20 hour week. The most efficient way of organising this would be to cut the number of days a week at work rather than the length of the working day. To even begin to achieve these levels, so that effective work sharing can take place, will require changes in attitude by several bodies. Governments will have to make it financially attractive for companies to implement such schemes, because today it is bureaucratically inefficient to employ two part-time workers when one full-timer will do. Trade Unions would also have to revise their attitudes and widen their areas of responsibility to include the unemployed as well as their paying membership. There are too many examples of groups of workers pressing for and getting overtime in communities that already have high unemployment. The third group which must reassess its situation is the work-force itself. Micro-electronics will improve productivity but a dramatic cut in the length of the working week may initially result in a drop in wages or, in present day conditions, pay increases that do not keep pace with inflation. A four day week is today a sign of economic ill-health, not a move towards full employment. It is doubtful whether much progress can be made without drastic changes in the industrial climate.

A second area on which a social policy must concentrate is the provision of effective retraining schemes and vocational education. If the new technology is to be wholeheartedly applied, many new skills need to be acquired and in so doing a large number of old ones will disappear. In the past, it was usual for an apprenticeship to give somebody a trade for life. It may now be that complete retraining will be necessary for most workers two or even three times during their working life. As Professor C. Freeman (1979) has pointed out, rapid technological change involves

> "The loss of old skills, jobs and workplaces and the organisation of new ones. If it is not to be accompanied by a great deal of misery and insecurity then it must be accompanied by greatly increased provision of re-training facilities and post-experience education."

As well as acquiring new skills for work, opportunities must also be created for wider educational involvement, sabbaticals, the prized perk of the university academic, should become more generally available and if the shorter working week becomes the norm, the development of leisure skills will gain importance. Leisure in this context incorporates all the activities not directly linked to one's main employment; they may well be educational, sporting, recretional, do-it-yourself or community work.

Following this there is the final main constituent of a social policy, namely improvements in the provisions for the so-called *caring industries:* Health, Education and Recreation. All these share a fundamental property in that the services they provide are unconditionally improved by decreasing the client/staff ratio. Rather than destroy employment, these industries have an almost infinite capacity for providing work. This is not to say that microelectronics will not be substantially used in health care, educational schemes and recreational pursuits but these uses will have no influence on the traditional benefits gained by moving towards a one to one ratio in nurse/patient, teacher/student or instructor/ pupil situations. Another feature common to these three industries is that in the past they have been mainly state financed and are by nature non-profit making. Private health care and education, by concentrating on particular members of the community, have been able to become financially viable but it is doubtful whether they could work, in their current form at least, without the existence of state schemes to train the personnel required.

If real improvements are to be made in the caring industries, substantial increases in Government spending are required without which very high charges would have to be paid for the services. The innovatory use of microelectronics will lead to increased productivity and higher profits, therefore if the whole community is going to benefit, the government must extract the appropriate taxes from the successful firms. Failure to do this will lead to a deterioration in public services which, if coupled with high unemployment, will produce an extremely unhealthy divergent society.

3.2.3 Investment and Innovation
When attempting to derive the most appropriate economic action that could be undertaken in Britain in order to alleviate the threat of mass unemployment, one should bear in mind the approach taken by other industrial countries. Although in the USA, West Germany, Japan and France inflation is still the main economic problem, there is an underlying belief that unemployment will eventually decrease and the best way to move harmlessly and speedily to this position is to invest heavily in the new technology. In doing so they hope to accelerate the creation of new jobs and increase their share of world trade thereby matching, as much as possible, the displacement of jobs.

In the USA there is a tradition of high private investment in new ideas and products. Tax concessions that protect risked capital encourages this approach and the Congress' 'Buy American' policy helps to consolidate it. A further factor is the high Defense budget which, as we have seen, fosters considerable development in advanced technology. Other countries have more direct Government involvement; by the beginning of 1980 West Germany's industries had obtained over £300 million for research and development. In Japan the figure is over £500 million, including a single grant of £32 million for an eight year project to develop a fibre-optics system that will replace conventional electronic communications in factories. Britain is far from this league. The National Economic Development Council (NEDC) gives some state support but plans, such as the £35-£40 million program of research and development in *opto-electronics,* has shown 'few signs of progress by the Government'. (NEDC 1980). Even the £70 million allocated to encourage chip manufacture has recently been cut to £55 million, despite the world shortage of basic memory chips, a shortage which could lead to our manufacturers being starved of a vital 'raw material' in more economically prosperous times.

Many informed observers have commented on what they consider to be the alarmingly low level of investment in new ideas in Britain. Here are just two quotes:
Lord Avebury (1978) – Chairman, DIGICO Ltd., 'Governments will have to put up the capital which the private financial institutions have been unable or unwilling to provide.'
Cabinet Office: Advisory Council for Applied Research and Development, (ACARD 1979), 'We recommend, therefore, that the Department of Industry should study how Government can foster the rapid development of new industries based on emergent technologies, in particular information technologies and biotechnology and of industries with high growth potential arising from the increasing need to conserve energy and materials.'

Historically, the UK has had an excellent record of Research but a poor one in terms of Development. The realisation of many potential new products will only take place when the convergent nature of micro technologies is understood. On its own, the chip has only a limited range or applications, but by amalgamating a number of processes such as telecommunications and data processing or digital control and biotechnology, considerable innovatory development can be engendered. The Department of Employment report, previously cited, highlights a shortage of electronic engineers and the 'absence of top mangerial interest in radical innovation' as reasons as to why Britain appears to be behind our industrial competitors in exploiting the opportunities arising from technological convergence. Shortages in skilled software personnel and engineers with both hardware and software knowledge are often quoted as further difficulties.

A cabinet Office report on Industrial Innovation recommends that the government should, amongst other things, give increased tax incentives for investments in new plant and machinery, make additional money available to the Science Research Council and Engineering Institutes for the support of manufacturing technology, and expand the Department of Industry Manufacturing Advisory Service. By appropriate planning, ample investment and the encouragement of innovatory practices (especially by individuals and small groups) it may be possible to pass through the 'unemployment phase' during our progression towards the post-industrial society with the minimum of personal hardship and social disruption.

3.2.4 Trade Union Response

Unfortunately, the first indication a work force often gets of new machinery being introduced is when it is actually being wheeled into the factory or office or, even worse, when the redundancy notices appear. As the most radical changes today tend to be ones centred on microelectronics, it is not surprising that many trade unionists have a very jaundiced view of the micro revolution. The TUC first debated the manpower implications of the new technology at their 1978 General Council which led, in the following year, to the preparation of a report *'Employment and Technology'* outlining a strategy for trade unionists when they negotiated what they term New Technology Agreements (NTAs). Recent experiences at Times Newspapers clearly illustrate the damage and resentment that can result if no satisfactory agreement is reached. They ceased publication for 11 months at an estimated loss to the company of £40 million.

The TUC document rejects 'the deterministic view that the advent of microelectronics must inevitably be associated with a particular level of unemployment.' It advocates a programme of action that includes many of the suggestions covered in the 'Social Policy' response, but it also spells out the following guidelines for NTAs:

1. Statutory right to full involvement in the drawing up of company plans and to representation on the policy board of the enterprise.
2. No new technology to be introduced until full agreement has been reached; status quo provisions; consultation prior to the decision to purchase.
3. Inter-union collaboration; negotiability of flexible demarcation lines; development of technical expertise by union representatives.
4. All relevant information to be made available to union representatives prior to any decision being taken.
5. No redundancies; redeployment of existing workforce; where inevitable, high redundancy payments.
6. Training and retraining provisions; lengthened redundancy periods used for retraining.
7. Reduction of working hours; elimination of overtime; longer holidays etc. Immediate aim is a 35 hour week.
8. Income levels should be maintained or improved; additional skills rewarded but improvements in conditions of service for all.
9. Union agreement over the level to which workers' performance is monitored; union involvement in the system design stage and subsequent reprogramming.

10. Provision of detailed guides on the health and safety adpects of particular equipment, such as Visual Display Units.
11. Procedures for reviewing progress; joint union/management study teams; trial period of operating; grievance procedures.

Many of the elements of this scheme have, for some years, formed a standardised union policy with particular reference to union involvement in decision making. It is, however, the feeling of the more involved unions, such as AUEW-TASS, ASTMS and APEX, that such agreements must be made before the use of microelectronic technology becomes widespread. At the same time, the bargaining potential of a union faced with a management intent on introducing such technology should not be underestimated.

3.2.5 The Scandinavian Experience

In Britain it would appear that, because of our history of confrontation and poor industrial relations, it could be extremely difficult to obtain agreements on the above points. Other countries have not experienced such problems; in Norway, for instance, the Federation of Trade Unions (LO) and the Employers Confederation (NAF) negotiated a general agreement on computer-based systems in May 1975. In is interesting to note that positive action by the Norwegian Computer Centre (NCC) was instrumental in setting up such agreements and that they continue to monitor its application, often being called in by the LO to offer technical advice. To give an indication of the flavour of the Norwegian agreement here are some extracts from the revised 1978 document:

1. ". . . it is important that computer-based systems are evaluated, not only from the technical and economic angles but also from social angles, so that all the aspects are taken into account in the development, introduction and use of such systems."

2. "Management will, through the shop stewards, keep their employees informed about all matters which are covered by this agreement."
   "Information will be given clearly and in a language easily understandable to those without specialist knowledge of the area concerned."
   "Furthermore, management and the shop stewards, both separately and jointly, will give the employees sufficient information for them to understand the fundamental features of the systems which they themselves either use or which affect them."
   "Also, employees who will be directly affected by new systems. . . should, to the greatest practical extent, be involved in the preliminary project work. . . . sufficient time will be allowed for this work, and both lost earnings and any expenses incurred in obtaining information will be covered."

3. "If the employees of an enterprise so desire, they may elect, preferably among the existing shop stewards, a special representative to safeguard their interests and to co-operate with management."

"The representative(s) will have access to all information on the hardware and software."

"Shop stewards and employees participating in actual projects will have access to all necessary documents."

"The enterprise will make sure that the special representative. . . is given the necessary training. . . . so that they may carry out their duties effectively."

It is worth re-emphasising two of the most important tenets of this agreement, firstly that computer systems must be judged by their social as well as economic and technical implications and secondly, although management must work closely with the shop stewards it is the responsibility of *both* groups to keep the employees informed.

In Sweden, although there has been no specific agreement about computer systems, the 'co-determination law' of January 1977 applies to this as well as many other topics. According to Paragraph 10 of this law, the union has the right to negotiate on all aspects of the enterprise, there being no restriction as to which issues can or cannot be raised. Moreover, Paragraph 11 forces the employer to automatically instigate negotiations when they plan 'important changes' to either the whole enterprise or to just the working conditions of a single employee. With this and the 'work environment law' the Swedish Trades Union Organisation has been able to negotiate local agreements on computer-based systems and, like their Norwegian counterpart, develop considerable skills and specialist staff in all areas of information handling. Building on this legislation, Nyygard at NCC and the Swedish DEMOS-project (Democratic Planning and Control in Industry) have both begun research aimed at analysing the potential for real industrial democracy, based on modern information processing equipment, 'right to know' agreements and trained employee representatives (Docherty 1980). It is no coincidence that the TUC's formula for a New Technology Agreement has so much in common with the Norwegian one. The Scandinavian experience here, as with other areas of contemporary computing, has set an example for the rest of the industrialised world. Unfortunately, it is not easy to visualise how such agreements would actually materialise in Britain, lacking as we do the sort of open society in which information is readily transferred, and with fewer analysts who have the same opinions on system design as those of the NCC.

It must be emphasised when dealing with the question of technological unemployment, that one cannot deduce any answer without reference to the general levels of unemployment and the prevailing economic and political climate. In spite of this, the advent of microelectronics might well be the final critical factor that causes a major re-evaluation of our attitudes to work and leisure. If this be the case, then detailed analysis of future trends, based upon realistic assessments of actual and envisaged technologies, will be vital if society is genuinely interested in alleviating the financial and psychological problems associated with not having a job.

3.3 TOMORROWS JOBS

The previous section considered the general impact of microelectronics upon employment levels. Overall trends and national policies were analysed. Micro-technology is such a diverse topic that it is difficult to describe the whole concept with any real accuracy. Of more practical concern is the assessment of actual applications in terms of their effects upon different sections of society. For example, although the combustion engine can be appraised in terms of power potential, it is not until it is fitted into a vehicle and subject to both enforced legislation such as speed and pollution limitations, and to an economic climate which will determine production costs, value and availability, that its real contribution to the whole community can be evaluated.

Considered below are a few actual or envisaged applications which highlight the groups of workers most likely to feel the immediate effects of technological innovations. The examples are taken from traditionally skilled, semi-skilled, commercial and clerical trades.

3.3.1 Mining

"In 1980 the National Coal Board (NCB) intends to introduce a computer control system in 24 pits at a cost of £10 million. The longer term aim is to equip 250 pits with the system, largely by the prophetic year of 1984. The NCB calls this new mine operating system Minos, named after the king of Greek mythology who had a minotaur in his maze of tunnels which he was determined to kill. Is this how the coal bosses see the jobs of the men in the mines? Or, is the NCB's central aim a major improvement in health and safety for miners?" (CSE 1980)

This quote asks a critical question; what are the objectives of this technology and whom do they serve? On one hand it could be to downgrade or replace miners, who collectively have more than once been something of a nuisance to the UK government. Alternatively, it could be a genuine attempt to improve or, in some cases, do away with one of the most dangerous jobs in the developed world. These objectives are not necessarily exclusive. In fact they may compliment each other, but the one which turns out to be the stronger motivator may only become apparent from the actual design of the automated process.

Minos is a complete mining system, incorporating some existing stand-alone equipment and other more experimental parts such as a management information service. At the coal face there is already considerable mechanisation. By the mid 1960's the Anderton Shearer Loader (ASL) had become the main tool of the face worker, and microelectronics has enabled the ASL to become automated although it still needs to be manually steered. The result of this innovation is two fold; firstly the driver can now be at the rear of the machine, instead of the head where the dust and spray is at its worst and the danger of lung disease greatest; secondly, fewer face workers are required. The Department of Employment (1979) have estimated that a typical coal face will soon see a reduction from twenty-two to fifteen jobs per shift. In addition, as the automated features of the ASL are improved, the skill and hence the authority of the worker will diminish. Once cut from the face, the coal must be cleared and again automated equipment is already in use, at Bagworth Colliery thirty conveyor belts and associated bunkers have been combined into a single working system. Minos will make full use of this technique as it will others, such as the linked environmental monitors which can trace the presence of gas in any part of the mine. When the coal reaches the surface, it will meet an automatic preparation plant similar to the one presently in use at South Kirby in Yorkshire. Here an £18 million investment has furnished a process that can deal with two million tons of coal from three collieries. This system is 'close-looped', or self-regulating, and requires only a minimal semi-skilled workforce.

Perhaps the most contentious aspect of Minos is its management information scheme, known in some mines as FIDO (Face Information Digestion On-line). Data are collected from all aspects of the miners' operations to give minute by minute information on such things as shift and face comparisons and the causes of any delay which might occur. All this information is displayed in the control room on the surface. With a fully operational Minos system, all production decisions will be taken in this control room and many processes will be automatically controlled from computers situated there. The equipment underground will tend to be dedicated machinery taking its instructions from the surface, and not from the mine-worker. Not surprisingly, the staff in the control room will not be members of the NUM — National Union of Mineworkers.

Minos will significantly change the balance of power in the mines. Whether one considers this to be a good or a bad thing depends on a number of personal factors beyond the scope of this book. It is undeniable, however, that with Minos the control of the technology will not rest with the worker who will actually use it, nor has the system been designed with their co-operation or consent. Face workers have a highly skilled, well paid job, which exposes them to a noisy, unhealthy and often dangerous environment where few people would wish to work. Microelectronics will decrease the number that have to and, for the remainder, provide a safer, cleaner outlook. Yet in assessing the full impact of Minos, the psychological effects upon the workers must also be taken into consideration. For the skilled worker, in whatever industry, job satisfaction must account for a great proportion of the overall rewards. To down-grade a skilled worker after perhaps twenty years of experience may involve deep emotional difficulties that must be balanced against potential improvements in his physical wellbeing.

In some ways mining represents an unusual example, for it is skilled workers who are feeling the adverse effects of microelectronics. Normally the highly skilled worker is the last to be affected by new equipment, because their tasks either cannot easily be replaced or genuine computer aids are provided for their assistance. Where automation and robotics hit hardest is in the semi-skilled sector, particularly in assembly line production. The most commonly quoted example of the 'new assembly line' is in the car making industry where manufacturers have made a virtue of their labour-reduced production. British Leyland (BL) and Ford UK are both heavily committed to such equipment for their new ranges of cars. The motivation for such an approach is competiveness and profitability, but in an industry plagued by poor industrial relations, there must also be the attraction of a less powerful shop-floor. The first Fiat factory to be automated was implemented at a cost of £3 million and allowed management to cut the workforce from 125 to 25, which represents a saving of £500 000 per year in labour costs. This implies a payback period of six years compared to the three years that is usual for robotic installations.

3.3.2 Textiles
One industry that has never been 'troubled' by poor working relations in the UK is textiles, nevertheless it is suffering considerably from strong international competition. Between 1973 and 1980 output from the woolen sector has fallen 30% and over 30,000 jobs have been lost, which is nearly one third of the 1973 total. The reasons for this decline are legion but two can be held chiefly responsible, poor productivity and misdirected marketing. The answer to the productivity position has been to invest in new technology in all sectors of the industry. Although textile manufacture involves different organisations with many work practices following traditional lines, one can highlight the following applications of microtechnology (TUCRIC bulletin, 'Wool Textiles', 1980).

Computer aided design equipment with special multi-colour, fine displays is becoming an increasingly necessary tool for the designer. This drastically reduces the time needed to develop the final design, thus removing a lot of the tedious aspects of the job. As productivity improves, a financial saving is realised by reducing staff. This happens throughout the production process and, although of great significance, it is not worth repeated mention at every stage. Stock control and warehouse management, if the firm is large enough, can also benefit from an automation scheme. In Japan especially, complete warehouse systems that do not require any staff inside are in operation. Loading and unloading at the entrance is the only human activity.

In attempts to improve efficiency most attention has been focussed on the weaving stage where sensors monitor faults in the fabric and attempt maintenance. Electronic patterns control the loom's action and fully controlled looms are now possible (estimated labour force required: one person per 120 looms). The next step could be to link the computer aided design computers directly to the production looms. During other processes, which go by such descriptive names as Blending, Carding, Combing, Twisting, Winding, Coating, Warping and Spinning, microprocessor based tools continually monitor quality and consistency, check faults and, where possible, optimise performance. In computer controlled dyeing, for example, only one tenth of a batch requires a second processing compared with a previous average of three dyes per batch. Another advantage is the increased flexibility which allows for small batch production and fibre variations at approximately half the cost of conventional dyeing.

Tailoring, too, has succumbed to computer involvement with Hepworths, the Leeds based firm, installing a £250,000 Charlie to handle bespoke tailoring automatically. Charlie's function is to cut patterns and its sophistication lies in the ability to extract the pieces required with a minimum of wastage. The quarter of a million pounds price tag reflects as much upon the software development as it does upon the equipment itself. Charlie has replaced fifty skilled cutters with six operators, and executes the job using about 6% less cloth. With such expertise it will repay its investment in under two years. Apprenticeship for skilled cutters normally lasts seven years, although in this particular case few new cutters have been trained by the industry in recent years. Charlie operates 30% of Hepworths bespoke production, although it is having difficulty with chequered cloth and unusual body measurements!

Control machinery is not cheap, woolcombing equipment alone has seen over £20 million invested. Once installed and working it must be exploited to its maximum potential so work is centred on the machines and many jobs are down-graded. More drastically, to get the most from this capital expenditure, work must continue 24 hours a day, preferably 7 days a week. Rather than free workers from boring anti-social work, the new technology can promote it. Job satisfaction is not one of the prime objectives of these new systems. The management view is, quite accurately, that without efficient production there will be no textile industry and no jobs over which to argue. But if microtechnology is so flexible, why not design industrial machinery to both optimise production and enhance worker involvement — at least for the employees who remain?

3.3.3 Banking

Whereas robots and automated production lines are a relatively new feature of the British industrial scene, the banking, insurance and financial sector of the economy has been involved with computers since its earliest days. The structual changes planned for these institutions will have as strong an impact on both employees and users as anything that is happening in industry. Before the introduction of computers into banking, a customer's account and the issuing of statements was done by hand and entirely by one's own branch. By 1960, most of the main banks had introduced mainframe computers to automate customers' accounts and because it was more economical to only have a few large computer systems, accounts were removed from the branches. Transactions were initially recorded on paper or magnetic tape and forwarded to the computer centre at the end of the day. Later, local terminals were introduced so that information could be sent directly to the computer. The branch manager was subsequently informed by post of all the previous days' transactions. As mainframes became more sophisticated, *on-line* interaction with the regional computer became possible. With this system a branch can now update a client's account automatically and have uptodate information on the state of all their customers. On-line transactions returned control to the branch manager although only in a limited way, for most transactions now involve cheques which are destined for other branches or different banks.

Clearing, which is the process by which banks return one another's cheques and balance the cash flow, was automated in 1968. Since then all cheques have had account numbers and bank and branch identification printed in magnetic ink so that computer controlled equipment can sort them correctly. In 1977, an international clearing centre was established called SWIFT (Society for Worldwide Interbank Financial Telecommunications). It is difficult to see how the modern banking system could manage without this type of equipment. Its use has considerably improved the productivity and hence usability of banks, to the extent that employment in this sector has increased throughout the 1960s and most of the 1970s.

Although dramatically improving the efficiency of our banks, mainframe computers have brought little change to the actual working structure of the high street branch, particularly from the customer's point of view. By contrast, microelectronics and improved telecommunications will alter things considerably. The first device which connected the client directly to the computer controlling his or her account, without the need for intermediate staff involvement is the *service till* or *cash point*. A spokesman for National Westminster made the following observation regarding the utility of these machines: (BIFU 1980)

"These Service Tills have been well accepted by customers and one sometimes sees queues at them, even when branches are open. To give an idea of the saving of cashier's time, over 8 million transactions were passed through the Service Tills in March this year (1979). At Bristol there were 10,000 transactions in one machine, which represents one every 4 minutes for 24 hours a day."

The interesting question here is how many of the eight million transactions represent existing bank usage and how many result from new business that the technology itself has generated. Are banks doing more work or merely rationalising the existing level? Cheque and service cards in the future will no doubt be combined and tills themselves will begin to appear in public places, removed from the bank wall. But these are only small changes, compared with the grander plans envisaged by the four big UK banks, for instance Lloyds have already opened what has been called a *lobby bank* in Luton. This branch is not only manned during the usual banking hours, but is also open from 8.00 am to 9.00 pm. It contains the latest cashpoint machines and a creditpoint, in which cash and cheques can be deposited. Many more lobby banks are planned. Coupled with this trend toward terminal based customer service is an increasing tendency to develop *satellite banking*. With this, many of the traditional functions of the 'high street bank' are hived off to specialised centres where the work can be undertaken on fully or partially automated systems. Local branches then become little more than a counter service which, as we have already seen, can be almost entirely automated. Even lending machines have been considered where credit can be requested and standard replies provided, with reference back to a manager if the computer does not have enough information to make a decision.

The technology for these new banking schemes is not complicated, all that is needed is a microcomputer capable of reading a customer's magnetically coded card, take commands from a simple keyboard and give out the required cash. The only complication is the difficulty of linking hundreds, and in the future thousands, of cashpoints to the one main computer so as to give a fast, reliable and accurate service. This multi-access mode of operation raises a number of problems, not the least of which is security. Computer crime is not a subject for this book, but it must be a factor of some importance in the design of an electronic money service, where the need for a totally secure and hence restrictive system has to be balanced against an easy to use, flexible one.

What are the important elements when assessing the impact of banking technology? The major one is, again, that of potential unemployment. In France it has been estimated (Nora 1978) that a 30-40% reduction in staff levels is expected. Similar predictions have been made for Britain and yet, at present only about half of the adult population use banks. If the new technology gives a more appropriate banking service then it is possible that this user level of 50% could rise to between 70% and 80%, thereby disproving predictions of mass unemployment (greater bank usage means more banking jobs). A major difficulty may again be one of timing. Automated banks could be a reality within five years but it will probably take twenty to thirty years before increased trade could cancel out this effect. For the staff that remain:

". . . it is evident to us that as a result of the new technology the following dangers face us in the Finance Industry.
(a) Loss of certain jobs.
(b) Loss of interesting jobs – those dealing with people.
(c) Reduction in promotion prospects and career opportunities.
(d) Loss of certain skills.
(e) Extended hours for computer staff and machine servicing staff.
(f) Security problems re: servicing machines.
(g) De-skilling of certain jobs." (BIFU 1980)

This is a very similar picture to that portrayed in the mining and textile industries – less interesting or skilled work and the need to adapt to the machine's way of working. In banking, the cause of these dangers is not microtechnology but the decision to adopt satellite banking. The mainframe represented the height of centralisation, the micro could, if so desired, put decision-making back in the hands of the local branches. Unfortunately, the re-establishment of local control has not been one of the major design motivations.

From the community's point of view, there are a number of features of these new banking methods which need to be considered. It must be of benefit to have 24 hour banks because the present restrictive opening hours make it very difficult for many people to get to a bank. Against this advantage, there are a number of possible drawbacks. Firstly, there is the question of the reliability of the equipment. Even with the longest queue inside the bank one is assured of eventually being served. This is not the case with an automated till which, no matter how good, will break down from time to time and with heavy use run out of money, especially over long holiday weekends. Secondly, one of the consequences of modern banking may be that the facility of being able to see your local manager to discuss financial matters disappears and no amount of automation will recompense this form of personalised communication. Finally, there is the problem of enforced participation, as more people use banks the trend of employers to pay directly into worker's accounts will increase, thereby forcing more and more people to use banks. This circle is of benefit to the banks but may not be to people not wishing to use cheque cards, cash points etc.

Banking methods form only one part of what has been called the cashless society, point of sale debiting and all its implications is but an extension of what has been outlined above. A full assessment of these systems is urgently required if the total impact on the community is to be predicted. Whilst automated systems only support existing banking practice then the problems may remain few. But if new systems are so efficient (for some elements of society), present facilities may disappear before the significance of such a move is fully appreciated. I have mentioned elsewhere that the demise of public transport is an example of this type of social change. Credit cards are another. When they were initially provided they were purely for convenience, saving people from carrying excessive amounts of cash around. Now, especially in the US, credit rating is a crucial social indicator and an increasing number of goods and services are obtainable *only* on credit. Fundamental changes in our banking systems effect not only those employed within that sector but many other working and non-working groups. It is critical that envisaged changes reflect the wishes of all members of society, because the issues go far beyond simple commercial profitability.

3.3.4 The Deserted Office
The term *'word-processor'* is now in common use in our language — even if there is disagreement on whether it is one word or two — and its implication for the standard typing pool is well understood. But the 'new' office goes a lot further than having just the odd word-processor:

"An 'automated office' is an office in which interactive computer tools are put in
the hands of individual knowledge workers, at their desks, in the areas in which
they are physically working." — Uhlig (1979)

Paper is an economically and environmentally expensive product and there is
no reason why it should remain the primary medium on which to store and
transmit information. Managers will have visual displays to replace documents,
filing will be done magnetically on computer controlled storage and, most
significantly, a comprehensive intercontinental telecommunication system will
transmit 'documents' from office to office and from city to city. Office productivity, which has hardly improved since the turn of the century, will increase
dramatically and have far-reaching ramifications upon employment.

As an example of the conflict which can arise out of the introduction of
office automation, consider the experience of a group of typists at Bradford
Metroploitan District Council. In 1976 a wide ranging review was undertaken to
analyse the effectiveness of various council departments; one of the recommendations, published in June that year, was that word-processor equipment should
be introduced into 'Jacob's well' typing pool. At the time the pool was manned
by 38 typists and 4 supervisors. The first these people heard about the proposed
changes was in April 1976, they had neither been consulted nor had taken part
in any feasibility study. The workers involved resented the imposition of this
new equipment and proposed strike action to back their position, NALGO, the
trade union involved, reluctantly supported this position but suggested that a
working party be set up with management to consider all aspects of the issue.
In February 1977 with NALGO'S agreement, the working party offered a
'natural wastage' deal which meant that no typist would be laid off and, additionally, no typist would be forced to work with the word-processors if they did not
wish to — they would be given alternative positions elsewhere. The original
management study had estimated that the manning level could be reduced from
42 to 15 with the new machines (11 typists, 2 seniors, 1 supervisor and 1 manager).
With NALGO support for the agreement, the women had little choice but to
accept the arrangement. The machinery was delivered in April 1977, training
started in May and it was in full use by July. After one year the workers' reactions
could only be described as disappointing. The women who decided not to work
with the new machines were generally given less interesting typing to do and the
word-processor operators themselves described their work as 'boring' because of
the diminished personal involvement. With the old system, a typist would have
responsibility for specific documents. She (they were all women) would type
the first draft, initial it, discuss changes with the author, correct it and produce
the final copy. Many wordprocessing units are organised to prevent such supposedly
time-wasting discussions; documents could be split between typists for collection
later and corrections undertaken by yet another typist. The 'author' can only
discuss changes with the supervisors or, at most, the seniors, not with the person
actually doing the work. This mode of operation is not a fundamental feature

of word-processors, and systems can be and have been designed to work on the more personal structure, giving greater overall satisfaction.

From the council's viewpoint, their first experience with office automation was not a success. Ill feeling was generated and the expected saving of £15,000 per annum was not realised. The unit probably saved something over £9,000 but when taking into account extra staff placed elsewhere, this figure drops considerably, perhaps even resulting in a loss. The equipment itself turned out to be far from perfect, the print paper was of a poor quality and the automated filing system allowing for retrieval of previously typed material was unreliable. This trouble can again be attributed to the lack of initial involvement of the workers who would actually use the equipment. If redundancy is one of the main motivations for implementing office automation how does one 'involve' the affected staff? (A report by Bradford Word-Processor Study Group on *the introduction of automated word processing systems* in Bradford Metropolitan District Council.)

Between 1979-80 the rate of unemployment amongst women in Britain grew at 47 times that for men. In automated production, banking and in the office, it is predominantly women who are being replaced by machines. A report from the Equal Opportunities Commission in October 1980 claims that up to 40% of all clerical jobs are at risk during the 1980s, implying that some 170,000 positions will be lost in under ten years. This serious situation can only be effectively countered by increased equal opportunities in traditionally male areas of training and work. This is a slow process that will not immediately alleviate the present imbalance.

A large proportion of office time is spent in answering or trying to reach someone via the telephone. British Telecom's System X will greatly assist this process. Of the many beneficial features that this new exchange equipment possesses, one of the most useful, for the office, will be the facility to redirect calls to either other personnel, an intelligent answering service or even to another location. Calling numbers will also be easier as two digit codes can be used for commonly rung destinations. With only a limited knowledge of available equipment, one can imagine an office in which the secretarial staff is much reduced, microcomputers control the filing of documents (computer files though, not a physical collection of paper) and the transfer and collection of electronic messages, and an automatic switchboard collates information from callers, forwarding the relevant data to the required person wherever he or she may be. Traditionally this person would be behind a desk, somewhere in the office, but in the future there will be little point in undertaking the time and fuel consuming journey to work. A terminal at home linked to the office computer system can supply him or her with all the office information required. Documents can be prepared on command and the telephone exchange will forward all calls. If a visit is necessary then this can just as well be made from home as from the office. An executive's base could easily be at the other side of the world as long as effective telecommunication links are maintained. Such a working arrangement already exists and must be expected to expand. Typists and secretaries, too, will work from home using their word-processors linked, again via the telephone network, to the office so as to obtain their instructions and 'return' completed work. Even the personal secretary, whose jobs includes organising the diary, answering the phone and preparing files, could be home based. Once the executive, the secretary, the typist and the clerk have been removed from the building then one is left with a mere information channeller, a deserted office.

The automated systems described here represent a formidably complex, yet critically important technology assessment. Their impact will affect the worker who loses his or her job, the worker who remains and the community at large. For the office staff there are obvious advantages from being able to work at home where they have more control over their own time. Some of the consequences to female employment may well be compensated by a changing work pattern whereby there could be a more equal split between work and family and the male and female roles. One must not, however, forget in this analysis that the homeworker has, since the industrial revolution, been the most exploited member of the workforce and physical isolation has always made it difficult to establish effective trade union representation. Increased unemployment, particularly among women, may persuade redundant office workers to operate from home. Straight-forward typing could become a cottage industry and there is even the fear that with global communication it would be possible to export typing requirements to areas paying what would be, to many, unacceptably low wages.

The main psychological problem associated with this form of work will arise because of the increased instances of people working in isolation. Most people want to get out of the house during the day, not to have to work there. For a large number of staff, the atmosphere in the office is a genuine source of comradeship which no amount of 'friendly' computers will replace. As physical travel becomes increasingly more expensive and telecommunications offer cheaper and easier alternatives, economics will dictate that fewer meetings should take place, instead there will be more electronic conferences — the linking of three or more people via the telephone system. One disadvantage of this electronically based society is the inherent problem of loneliness resulting from such cloistered communications.

Undoubtedly one of the real benefits of computer-centred office equipment, which would be felt by everyone, is the increased efficiency that such systems should bring. 'Should', because the micro can be used to cut through bureaucracy or, conversely, present yet another obstacle to free information flow. Which of these options will be realised depends upon who controls the technology and whom it is really intended to benefit. When considering the consequences of the deserted office, it is attractive to look to the demise of the early morning and late afternoon rush hours. But what happens to the vast inner city office blocks and the infrastructure that is built around a concentration of office workers?

The word-processor will hit not only the typing pool but the local shops and cafés. If office automation becomes a reality on any sort of scale then it must disturb the existing work order. Whether it does or not will depend not on the technology, for that is already available, but on management innovation and motivation.

3.4 THE INDIVIDUAL AND THE INFORMATION SOCIETY

Because employment plays such a central role in our society it is understandable that the short and medium term effects of microelectronics on job levels has been the crucial question on which any social assessment of computers is based. Another issue which generates similar alarm and which may, in the long term, be of far greater concern is Information Technology and the effects it will have upon personal liberty and privacy. Since larger computers became available the trend for storing data electromagnetically has been gaining popularity. With the cheap micro and the refinements in telecommunication techniques, equipment can now hold and manipulate vast quantities of data and be interrogated by VDUs situated miles from the actual machine. Moreover, an increasing number of these large data processing computers are being integrated into national and international networks. Local authorities, various departments of central government, tax offices, police and security services, and some employers, make full use of computers to hold assorted information on all citizens. The vehicle licensing centre at Swansea is one of the more publicised government run computer centres which, although it acquired a poor reputation in its early days, is now working much more efficiently.

In addition to all these agencies there are also many private security and finance institutions who hold information on members of the general public and there are the many surveys and questionnaires which gather data on large groups of individuals. All these activities build a network of information covering every man, woman and child, which is then stored for future reference on computers. In Britain, for example, more than half the adult population (about 22 million) are now on police files; in the future, the National Health Service and the tax office will almost certainly computerise their records. In view of the available technology and the above applications, the question of whether one can protect personal privacy in an information based society becomes of paramount importance. As well as the problem of protecting computerised files on individuals, there is the more sinister danger of one's everyday activities being monitored either by the state, one's employer or a commercial competitor. In describing the 'pessimistic' view of the micro, instances of word-processor and supermarket cash till abuse were cited, which illustrated that surveillance at work is already a feature of the micro age.

On a more systematic level, British Telecom's System X exchange is designed to allow 'official' telephone tapping. Calls destined to be 'overheard' can be routed to special centres, run by either the Home Office or British Telecom; no physical action is required, the software has been written to accommodate such requests.

In order to determine whether modern information systems constitute a threat to the privacy of an individual, the concept of 'privacy' needs to be understood. This is a suprisingly difficult task, and no national legislation has ever defined it; yet privacy is held sacrosanct by free societies and violated by totalitarian regimes. In an increasingly integrated community it is obvious that certain organisations will need to hold centralised information on members of the public. Manual systems with card indexes and cross references have existed for some time and been accepted by the majority of society. Why then is there an outcry against the prospect of using a computer rather than a filing cabinet? The reasons for this reaction might be based upon the appreciation that, although the data concerned may be identical, the method of processing it is not. Manual systems can not be interrogated from a distance and once the volume of data exceeds a certain limit they become slow and unwieldy — therefore there is no advantage in linking together different indexes. Moreover, they only allow a very simple cross referencing. The natural constraints of this system are the protectors of our privacy. Early computerised methods, because of limited software and hardware, were also 'inefficient'. By comparison, access to a modern computerised data base can be made via a telephone line from anywhere. They are fast and can also be linked to other such systems to give powerful cross referencing.

Although privacy is difficult to define, it implies the right to withhold specific aspects of one's life from certain people. For example, although it is perfectly proper for one's doctor to keep a detailed account of your health, it is unacceptable for employers to do likewise. Similarly, though an employer knows about your work, one would not expect friends and family to be party to such information. The tax office knows a great deal about your personal circumstances, but this data is not generally available to other government departments: protection for an individual is secured because of the lack of information flow between these diverse groups. This returns us to the question of the existence of such protection in the future, when the technology will allow the easy exchange of such data. The National Council for Civil Liberties, UK (NCCL) has isolated four key aspects of the information business: (NCCL 1968)

1. The way in which personal information is collected.
2. The use of inaccurate, out of date or irrelevant information or opinions as the basis for decisions.
3. Inadequate security to ensure that confidential information is kept that way.
4. The transfer of information given for one purpose without an individual's consent.

English law has not dealt adequately with these aspects and with microtechnology they will become an even greater source of concern. The Younger report (Cmnd 5012) of 1972 on privacy has the following to say about computers:

> "We cannot on the evidence before us conclude that the computer as used in the private sector is at present a threat to privacy, but we recognise that there is a possibility of such a threat becoming a reality in the future."

After this report the Home Office published a White Paper, *Computers and Privacy*, which advocated the setting up of a committee on Data Protection to advise on the structure of a possible Data Protection Authority and associated legislation. This committee, under Norman Lindop, reported in December 1978 (see below for details of report). Since then government has not brought forward the legislation necessary to set up a Data Protection Authority. By comparison, Sweden introduced such legislation in 1973, the US (for its own citizens only!) in 1974, West Germany in 1976, Canada in 1977 and France in 1978. Additionally, the following countries have passed legislation: Australia, Austria, Denmark, Holland, Luxembourg, New Zealand, Norway, Portugal and Spain. In Britain it has been left to the National Computer Centre (NCC) to attempt to organise and monitor personal data processing systems such as the 1981 census.

3.4.1 The Lindop Report

In keeping with the practices of many other countries the Lindop report, because of difficulties in defining 'privacy', has recommended that rather than establish rights under law there should be a set of codes of practice based upon a set of principles. The codes of practice are to be administered by a Data Protection Authority, DPA, who not only set up the codes but also police their adherence and give general advice. An important element in the recommendations of the Lindop report is that the DPA should report directly to Parliament, not to a minister, and that its members be appointed by the Crown with its activities scrutinised by a parliamentary committee. It must be both independent and seen to be independent of governmental control.

The Seven Principles

The general principles that the DPA must accept as self-evident are split into three groups of interest, those of the community at large, those of the data users, and those of the data subjects (i.e. the individuals on which data is being stored).

> *'In the interests of data subjects*
> (1) Data subjects should know what personal data relating to them are handled, why whose data are needed, how they will be used, who will use them, for what purpose, and for how long;
> (2) Personal data should be handled only to the extent and for the purposes made known when they are obtained, or subsequently authorised;

(3) Personal data handled should be accurate and complete, and relevant and timely for the purpose for which they are used;
(4) No more personal data should be handled than are necessary for the purposes made known or authorised;
(5) Data subjects should be able to verify compliance with these principles;

In the interests of users
(6) Users should be able to handle personal data in the pursuit of their lawful interests or duties to the extent and for the purposes made known or authorised without undue extra cost in money or other resources;

In the interests of the community at large
(7) The community at large should enjoy any benefits, and be protected from any prejudice, which may flow from the handling of personal data." (Cmnd 7341).

How the DPA Would Work

The DPA is primarily concerned with data processed by automatic means and does not deal with manual systems — a fact lamented by the NCCL. A user of personal data must register with the DPA and state the nature of the data involved and the methods and reasons for processing it. The DPA will then, depending on the type of activity specified, relate the rules or codes under which the user must operate. Failure to do so would invoke legal sanctions.

'National security' is a cloak often used to conceal and excuse actions by the police and security forces. Lindop discussed at length the role of the police computers and decided that they should be subject to the authority of the DPA and recommended that it should be possible for:

". . .at least one senior official of the DPA to have a security clearance sufficient for him (sic) to be able to operate in effect as a privacy consultant to the Home Office and the security services."

This view was not entirely endorsed by the Police; the Metropolitan Police refused to give any evidence to Lindop. West Germany has one of the most extensively computerised security services, having expressly excluded such work from their Data Protection Act. The Lindop report further recommended that no universal personal identifier, UPI, should be allowed to evolve either conciously or informally. A UPI is a system whereby all citizens are given a unique code number which they use in all transactions with government bodies. This would so facilitate the collection of information on any individual, perhaps from a number of different data bases, that it was felt to be a potential danger. The idea here is that privacy is best protected if stored information is widely distributed and not easily brought together.

3.4.2 Police Computers

In dealing with computers operated by police forces, the committee drew a clear distinction between public records concerned with *information* and those of *intelligence*. Information is considered to be hard factual data such as date of birth, previous convictions, car registration and number, and so on; intelligence, on the other hand, is subjective in nature, implying an interpretation of factual evidence. The blurring of the boundary between these two types of data caused great concern to the committee who commented that:

> "The linking of factual personal information about an identifiable individual with speculative data about criminal activity could pose a grave threat. . ."

Before 1960 the police were concerned solely with information appertaining to convicted criminals. After this date their area of interest was extended to include suspected or suspicious individuals, in what is generally known as pre-emptive policing. The collecting and collating of intelligence is now a recognised activity of all police forces. In addition to criminal activities, the Special Branch ' monitors four further categories: (Ashman 1979)

1. Those suspected of espionage in the ultimate employ of a foreign power.
2. Those suspected of terrorism.
3. Those employed by the State in sensitive areas, MPs, leading businessmen and those in the media.
4. Those considered subversive.

The definition of subversive was originally that given by Lord Denning in 1963 and stood for those who 'would contemplate the overthrow of government by unlawful means' (Cmnd-2152). This was later changed by the Home Secretary, Mr Rees, in 1978 to mean:

> 'Those activities which threaten the safety or wellbeing of the State, and are intended to undermine or overthrow parliamentary democracy by political, industrial or violent means." (Hansard April 1978)

The police use a computerised record system at both local and national level. In 1969 it was decided to create a £35 million Police National Computer, PNC, which is now in operation at Hendon. This PNC serves about 300 terminals around the country and holds information on fingerprints, wanted and missing persons, and stolen vehicles. It also has over 19 million records on vehicle owners from the vehicle registration computer at Swansea. This information helps the police to prevent crime but at the expense of holding data on the majority of the adult population. The Home Office has said that this computer will not be linked to other government computers or to criminal intelligence systems which, at face value, implies that the Home Office recognises the distinction between information and speculation. Unfortunately in practice this distinction is less clear. For example, on the vehicles files of the PNC there is space to provide additional information about each car, under three categories:

SUS — Suspicion of being used in crime.
POL — Being used for police work.
INT — Of long term interest to the police.

There have been a number of cases in the last few years to indicate that political associations such as the Anti-Blood Sports League are noted on vehicle records. The Home Office has confirmed this and and has described the criteria by which information is put onto the computer — 'when a police officer has judged it relevant'. This is exactly the situation that the Lindop committee were concerned about. By comparison, 'Police Review' described the changes in the following way:

> "Police intelligence is now forward-looking, anticipating who is going to commit what, when and where, and because it is so purposeful it is also frequently libellous . . .Much of the information is personal details of a suspect, his family, associates, way of life and although it may seem to trespass on the freedom of the individual it is the bread and butter of successful policemanship." (see Bunyan 1979)

One of the more blatant intelligence systems is run by the Metropolitan Police Force; over 1.5 million people have records on this computer, many of whom do not have criminal records. The Special Branch use it for the categories previously mentioned and such groups as suspected illegal immigrants, drug traffickers and even victims of crime. The data base which stores this information is managed so as to give comprehensive cross referencing; for example it would take only seconds to trace each person who has been in contact with a certain MP in the last six months, has red hair and lives in Basingstoke.

The problem with computerising this type of system is that there is no longer a natural restriction on the amount of data entered. A manual system can only take so much before it becomes unworkable and therefore care is taken to select only the important data for storage. With a computer system, the tendancy is to record all manner of third hand, out of date and sometimes blatantly inaccurate information; as the 'Police Review' admits:

> "Much of this information is valid intelligence. A substantial proportion is unchecked bunkum."

Not only is data unchecked as it is entered on a computerised system but there is also the psychological power of the information when it comes out. Computer aided analysis seems much more plausible and convincing than an officer's 'hunch' or some observations in a PC's notebook. In addition to the confidence most people place in sophisticated machines there is less inclination to challenge computer produced data and, more importantly, less motivation to remove erroneous information. By leaving inaccurate and hearsay evidence on any individual, there will come a time when a perfectly law abiding citizen has such a long file that their involvement in some illegal activity will be assumed by any officer viewing his or her 'record'.

The assessment of police information systems is complex; some people take the view that if you have nothing to hide, you have nothing to worry about. Others fear police harassment over perfectly legal activities or associations, such as being a member of a political party. Over-zealous interpretation of computerised information has already been illustrated in one extreme case where a juror was barred from service because the PNC had recorded that he was the *victim* of a crime. Perhaps the most pressing need in this electronic era is for the police computers themselves to be policed from outside the force, with codes of practice being laid down by a data protection authority.

One example that can be seen as a small step in the appropriate direction has been taken by Northumbria police. Here, information entered onto the computer is only stored for re-use after it has been checked by a senior officer and, even then, the 'intelligence' is awarded a limited time span after which it will be automatically removed from the system. For very sensitive information, the computer will merely point to its existence, the actual data being stored in a centralised manual system under close control. Although this may only be a cosmetic feature to boost public confidence, it does have the effect of re-asserting one of the old constraints on data storage that protected our privacy in the past.

3.4.3 The Swedish Experience

To give an indication of how data protection legislation would work, one must look to countries that already have such laws. Sweden passed its first Data Act in 1973 and after many years of experience is presently proposing a second major act. However, before considering their example some background knowledge of Swedish society may prove helpful. Much was made in the US of their recently passed Freedom of Information Act; in Sweden they have had such a principle for over 200 years. It is a cornerstone to their democracy, with all government documents, except those pertaining to a narrowly defined area of national security, being accessible to everyone. A second important facet of Swedish life is that they are heavily computerised; on average each adult will have information stored about her or him in over a hundred different computer files. These two factors no doubt explain why Sweden was one of the first nations to tackle the problem of upholding privacy in an information age.

Their 1973 Act set up a Data Inspection Board, DIB, an autonomous authority which administers the Data Act independently. The Lindop committee obviously took the DIB as its model for the Data Protection Authority. The Board is an eleven man/woman directorate, comprised of representatives from the various parliamentary parties, the business community, trades unions and other interested groups. Their main brief is to register users (or keepers as they are called), obtain agreements on the *directives* under which they will process information and then grant permission for the processing to take place. The directives are flexible, in that they are shaped to fit each particular application. This is in contrast to the proposed British method which would only allow some fifty codes of practice. The Data Inspection Board works on the principle that absolute privacy is not possible in a modern society, that infringements are inevitable but they must not be allowed to undermine personal liberty. Data users are subject to many restraints; every single data file containing personal information must be registered with the DIB and the reasons for storing the data noted. Two separate files cannot be concatenated without permission and new uses of the data are subject to re-registration.

This, unfortunately, led to the odd anomaly; for instance a Christmas card list containing names and addresses of friends and relatives, even if held on a personal home computer, would need, in theory, to be registered. Word-processors however, which temporarily hold information before printing out verbatim, are normally considered to be outside the provisions of the Act. Large data bases are usually only licensed to collect information of a personal nature if the following conditions are met:

1. Those who are going to be registered are members, employees or customers of the responsible keeper or have some other comparable association with the keeper.
2. Those who are going to be registered give their consent thereto.

In keeping with traditional Swedish legislation, individuals can request to be notified of all information held about them and obtain this free of charge. It is the responsibility of the keeper to ensure that data is correct. If for any reason an item of personal information is suspected of being incorrect, the keeper must take steps to verify it and make whatever alterations are necessary to improve its accuracy. This includes not only deleting or correcting existing items but also the addition of extra information where this will promote a truer picture of the person. Even medical records are open to scrutiny, doctors must take specific action to withhold information from a patient and only then for a limited period and in the patients interest. This applies whether records are computerised or not.

The DIB can further restrict the activities of keepers. This includes imposing a time period over which data can be used. This particularly concerns statistical surveys, and the control of what happens to the data files once they have fulfilled their original purpose. The reason for this latter power is to prevent personal data files becoming a commodity that can be bought and sold, or being part of a company's assests which would be transferred (along with the furniture) if the business were sold or ceased to trade.

Monitoring
The DIB should not be seen as purely a licensing agent. Its role also includes monitoring compliance with the Act and being an information and complaints service for the general public. Because of these requirements, members of the

DIB are entitled to inspect all computer centres where there may be personal data handling, in order to uncover any unfair infringement of personal privacy (Freese 1978).

Failure to comply with directives, register personal data files or to allow free access is an offence which can incur either a fine or up to one year of imprisonment. The Data Act has, in fact, created a new category or criminal offence, namely *Data Trespass* which means the unlawful use or alteration of personal data. Imprisonment for this misdemeanour can be up to two years. Probably the main deterrent to improper use has been the power invested in the DIB to confiscate misused or unregistered files. Undoubtedly computer systems could be designed that would make it very difficult to ensure accordance with the act but the DIB has no power to restrict the use of any such systems.

Organisation Cost

The DIB employs less than 30 staff, of which 20 have decision making responsibility. It has a budget of around £400 000, a proportion of which comes from the licensing fee. This is of some concern to statistical bureaux and research departments in universities who find themselves having to pay for a license. By January 1979 the DIB had received 24,000 applications appertaining to approximately 30,000 personal files, and had managed to cope chiefly by adopting a non-bureaucratic approach. Lindop estimated that the real cost of his Data Protection Authority would be £500 000. The government considered this too expensive, which is possibly one reason why the DPA has yet to appear in Britain.

The New Swedish Data Act

The original Act has now been in force for a number of years, and reviews and further legislation have been formulated which modify the original provisions. The DIB appears to have worked well and many organisations who were originally sceptical about the Board are now satisfied by its implementation. Yet a significant number of people are far from convinced that their privacy is being upheld. Part of the problem stems from the inevitable conflict between the right to privacy and the public's right of access to government information and statistics which, by their very nature, are of great commercial value.

Two areas covered by the new act are the right of trade unions to influence the content of personal files, and the control of automatic surveillance of an employees' work standards, a subject not covered by the 1973 Act. Another dissatisfied group is the social scientists who consider it costly and time consuming to have to gain approval from the DIB for their every action. In these circumstances, the DIB has been criticised for acting as a censor of research, an activity beyond its mandate. Perhaps a real cause of remaining public scepticism is the lack of confidence people have in the ability of the DIB to stand up to cabinet and parliament. Under the 1973 legislation, the DIB cannot veto the creation of a government file (although it can exercise some control over it). Unfortunately it is precisely in this area that the individual feels most vulnerable. In Denmark, the equivalent of the DIB has total control over government files, Britain must decide whether or not to follow this example.

Another aspect of data protection concerns that of 'group privacy'; an individual may well be more hurt by information about a group or association to which she or he belongs, than by any misuse of personal data. This is a difficult area to tackle but a natural progression from personal protection, in that information concerning a group must reflect on the members of that group, be it political, recreational or financial. Finally the proposed Act looks at the increasing problem of *soft data* on computing systems, an aspect deemed insignificant by Sweden in 1973, but which has received full attention in the more recent Lindop report. Soft data is defined as meaning value judgements or opinions of one human being about another. Lindop called this intelligence:

> "An enticing quality of automatically produced data is that they so often give the impression of being much more precise than they are, or than manually produced data. . .'The computer has said so, so it must be true, anyway we can't change it' — how many times have we been told this by government and by business?" (Aner 1978).

These are some of the observations made about data protection after many years experience of legislation. Countries such as Britain which have not yet formulated laws, would be wise to learn from these endeavours.

3.4.4 Britain Without Data Protection

The Lindop committee presented its report to the Home Secretary in 1978. Even if the present government decide to bring forward the necesarry White Paper and act upon its recommendations, it would still be two to three years before a working Data Protection Authority could be established, because such things as the Codes of Practice would take time to develop. The present government does not appear to consider data protection legislation an important issue and because the DPA would require some central funds there is every possibility that we shall go through the whole of the present parliament without a Data Protection Act. One might expect that this would benefit data processors became it relinquishes them of the task of having to register and describe their operations. Many international and exporting companies, however, are concerned about the potentially harmful effects brought about by the absence of a British Act.

The drawback to national legislation (which was recognised in Sweden and all other nations which have passed a personal data protection act) is that illegal data processing activities could take place overseas in countries where such conduct is not proscribed. These are known as *data havens* and Britain is rapidly becoming one of the last in the developed world. Nations have protected themselves against these havens by making it illegal for trans-border data flow to take place between themselves and any country not already covered by an adequate data protection Act. Many British firms have already lost business because we do not have the appropriate legislation and in many areas of research and medicine Britain could find itself increasingly isolated, since such systems as in international automatic kidney donor matching scheme inevitably require some personal data to be held on a computer. If legislation is passed in Britain, it will be because of pressure exerted by the international business sector.

With an increasing activity in trans-national data exchange, the supervision of national laws is becoming very difficult. The EEC is considering a European Convention which would formulate a common approach to the rights of the individual in this sphere of information handling. In many ways their proposals go further than the Lindop report, facilitating public access to files held by any member country. Thus if business cannot convince the Home Office of the need to legislate, the EEC might well force Britain to adopt an overall plan. Meanwhile, the obtaining of legislation and agencies such as the DPA is only one small step towards the protection of our privacy. Britain has, by nature, an insular society and one specific Act of Parliament will not alter this. However well the DPA is constituted it will still be an extension of the state. Confidence in its ability will grown only when it is fully functioning and seen to be efficient.

Because of the inherent inefficiency of manual data processing systems, their influence is very limited. No such constraints exist for computerised systems, however, therefore external restrictions must be imposed. The solution must be to design information technology in such a way that it works within existing ordinances; data base software and telecommunication organisations must reflect the wishes of the law and make abuses easier to detect. Trade Unions agreements invariably stipulate that employers do not use new technology to monitor a worker's performance. But only by being involved in the design stage will they be able to satisfy themselves that such activities would be impossible. The degree to which the public uses any information technology will very much depend upon their belief that it will not lead to undue violation of what they consider to be their right to privacy.

3.5 BOOKS, NEWSPAPERS, TELETEXT AND VIDEOTEX

The protection of privacy, although crucial, is not the only significant factor when considering the role of the individual in an information society. As important as safeguarding one's own personal facts and data is the right of access to what has been called *public knowledge;* to keep informed of local authority and central government activities; to be aware of ones rights under the law; to know to what extent industrial processes are polluting the atmosphere or consuming raw materials; to be able to examine alternative economic and social philosophies; to have access to uncensored news media etc. To acquire information is to accumulate wealth and to control information is to have power. Dictatorships are synonomous with close control over public knowledge; the burning of books and the closure of newspapers are the hallmarks of an oppressive regime. By comparison, democracies should be, but are not always, associated with wide access to information.

That information is of value is evident if one examines the role of the professions in our society, many of which are mere custodians jealously guarding their particular field of knowledge. How would solicitors earn a living if the general public had free access to well documented, easy to use, law guides. What would accountants do if the tax laws were simplified? Even some medical practitioners prefer to work behind a cloud of mystery which we as consumers must respect and never violate. One facet of any profession, be it doctor, lawyer, engineer or computer scientist, is that those already qualified control the methods by which others may join. Whilst obstacles such as examinations and length of training protect the 'standards' of the profession, they often hinder public understanding.

Information is the key to the professions but, more importantly, it is central in determining the brand of democracy under which we live. In Britain, we have already had one example of devolved government, the referendum on our continued membership of the EEC; were we all well enough informed to make such a decision? Many European Countries have had referenda on the issue of nuclear power, and Britain may also be forced by public pressure to 'put it to the people'. But can we be sure that a debate between 'Friends of the Earth' enthusiasts and a multimillion pound state-controlled industry would give the public enough information to make their own decisions? In the USA, the State of California has had a large number of *propositions* to test public reaction in all manner of subjects including whether it is right for people to smoke in public and the possibility of halving local taxes. Is it public knowledge or prejudice that has governed these polls?

Traditionally, after a period of school education and, for some, college or university, our knowledge is drawn from books, newspapers, radio and television, our personal endeavours and social interactions. Many views about the future predict the demise of the printed word; so it is perhaps of value at this point to list some of the features which characterise the more common forms of this medium:

1. Open to all — only prerequisite is the ability to read.
2. Inexpensive — especially if libraries are used.
3. Local, national and international topics are covered.
4. Size of work is no real restriction.
5. Libraries contain conflicting contributions, even if individual books and newspapers are consistent.
6. Although categorisation and indexing are employed, browsing is a natural and useful activity, both through a book or newspaper and along a shop or library shelf.

7. The acquistion of material can be very time consuming, newspapers may come through the front door but good libraries and bookshops can be some distance away.

In particular areas of knowledge, the growth in the mass of printed material available has stretched the traditional publication system to breaking point. In microbiology, approximately 150 new papers are published everyday, because it is impossible for any single person to keep abreast of all this information, researchers specialise. To help them find the publications of interest, titles of papers together with brief descriptions (abstracts) are made available periodically, but even scanning through these lists can pose insurmountable problems for all but the very specialised. One solution has been the establishment of a large computer retrieval system on all microbiological publications. Authors of papers list the *keywords* that best indicate their area of study, the computer system stores these 'pointers' and when a research worker calls for all publications containing a certain combination of keywords, a list is produced and, at a cost, sent to him. This is just one example of an electronic imformation system. Its function is to help people keep more up to date and by having more information available, the pressure to specialise is lessened. Microbiology is an extreme case but it is not atypical; computerised information equipment is now found in all walks of life. The United Nations Environmental Programme has set up an international referral system for sources of environmental information (Infoterra), the purpose of which is to disseminate data on 'environmentally sound' industrial and agricultural developments. This new but already effective system would be impossible to organise without the use of a computer-operated directory at the Activity Centre in Nairobi.

The French were among the first nations to recognise the significance of linking together automated systems and information. They devised the now universally accepted term *informatique* (anglicised as *informatics*) which describes such technologies in the widest sense. In the public domain, two distinct systems have been devised – *teletext and videotex*.[†] The former necessitates the use of spare lines on the existing TV channels to broadcast *pages* of information that fill the ordinary television screen. The BBC's version is called *Ceefax* (see facts) and consists of a dual system on their two channels. The IBA's technically identical version has been named *Oracle* (Optional Reception of Announcements by Coded Line Electronics). To use either of these, certain equipment is required, namely an adapted television and a small hand-held control box similar to the portable controllers that are already available on many sets. A significant restriction of teletext is that there is no user interaction; pages are broadcast in rotation at the rate of about four per second and the user must 'grab' a page as it appears on the screen and hold it on the set in order to

---

† Radiotext is a third system but has not received much attention as yet.

look at it. This inevitably means an inherent restriction on the number of pages that can be made available because consumers might not be prepared to wait minutes until the required information arrives. At present, Ceefax and Oracle operate with about 200 pages. The maximum proposed number is 800, which would take more than three minutes to scan. The type of information available on these systems includes news headlines, stock exchange indexes, sports results, entertainment guides and transcripts of broadcast programmes for the hard of hearing.

By comparison, videotex is interactive because it uses telephone lines rather than broadcasts. A user can ask for a page directly without having to wait for it to 'pass by'; there is therefore no limit to the number of pages available, making it theoretically possible for a complete information system to be structured. The first public videotex system to come into general use was the British Post Office's (now British Telecom) Prestel. *Viewdata* was the original name the Post Office used but when they tried to register it the Patent Office decided that it was too all-embracing a title and so *hey Prestel*! However attempts to have viewdata accepted as the generic name were thwarted hence *Videotex* became the international tradename.

3.5.1 Prestel

Prestel was developed in the early seventies and the first experimental system was inaugurated in September 1975. From the outset, the object of Prestel was seen to be threefold; to be profitable, to provide an expansion of jobs in an industry feeling the effects of microelectronics more than most and,

> "Thirdly, Prestel has a public service objective – the provision of a value-for-money, socially useful, enjoyable communications and information retrieval system that can be used by large numbers of people at work, at home, all round Britain, without editorial intervention by the Post Office as carrier." – Hooper (1980), director of Prestel.

The data Prestel makes available are stored on a series of regionally based, medium sized computers. The users communicate with these data bases using ordinary telephone lines and the information appears on a converted television. A complete screen consists of twenty-two lines each with a maximum of forty characters. The consumer controls the operation with a portable hand-set containing a numeric pad like that of a calculator.

The following are a small sample of the many roles already envisaged for Prestel: instant newspaper, encyclopedia, consumer guide, mail order house, message service, booking office, travel agent, professional advice centre, electronic mail, local authority and central government publicity medium, education aid, electronic notice board, information gatherer for public enquiries, codes of practice publisher (such as The Health and Safety at Work legislation), recreational facility, software source, British Rail Timetable, instant ballot box, advertising, etc.

If they are available in your area, the cost of obtaining these services (1981) would entail a £500 conversion to your television set (likely to be reduced to around £100 as the system becomes well established); £12 for a socket extension plus the additional rent, the rate for a local call plus 3p per minute during the day (3p per 3 minutes at other times) and a page charge for the particular data you require. The page charge is variable — some, which are deemed to be public notices, are free whilst others range from a half-penny to 50p with some specialist information costing up to £100. A page, once obtained, can be held indefinitely on the screen with no further connection charge. The costs are high, no doubt reflecting the prime objective of Prestel 'to be profitable', so initial customers will mainly be from businesses,[†] although there is mounting pressure on local authorities to site Prestel stations in public places. A university library has calculated that its Prestel system adds only one tenth of a per cent to its budget and local libraries could well install coin-operated sets to make the services available to the general public.

Information on Prestel is, as with Ceefax and Oracle, organised into pages, of which there are at present 156,000 with a total of 500,000 envisaged by the mid-eighties, compared with the 200 or so available via teletext. Pages are linked together in a tree structure with any one page having up to ten pointers which indicate to the user other relevant pages that she or he may wish to refer to. These pointers give a coherent structure to the data base which would otherwise be just a list of half a million pages; but who decides which pages are relevant to others? For example, should a page of mail order offers be linked to the appropriate consumer guide for the goods or even to other mail order firms selling the same products?

The user's hand held set has a number of functions, the most straightforward of which are:

Jump to indicated page
Recall previous page
Recall present page (for use in cases of bad transmission)
Return to top of selection tree

With these instructions the user can look at whichever pages she or he wishes and in any order. Any particular page may consist of a number of frames, each of which will fill the screen, once a page has been indicated the Prestel system will jump directly to it, the frames are then viewed in sequence.

One important feature of any videotex system containing a hundred thousand pages or more is its index. Prestel employs an intentionally simple method in order to create a non-technical 'friendly' interface, but many users have criticised

[†]By October 1980 just over 6,000 sets had been sold for Prestel use compared with the 50,000 envisaged by BT.

its limited scope; other systems have assumed that participants are already conversant with computerised devices and have a reasonable level of keyboard skills. The index pages are free for the consumer to consult although there is always the cost of the telephone call. Another facility available on nearly all videotex systems is for transmitting and receiving information via the telephone line. At present (1981), Prestel only supports a very limited form of communication which sets aside particular pages on to which the consumer can put numerical messages. Initial use has been restricted to ordering goods from mail order firms, entering competitions or booking holidays. This is an important aspect of information systems which will be returned to later.

Having discussed Prestel from the user standpoint, there remains one area as yet not considered; how does information get onto the data bases in the first place? British Telecom run the system in the sense of operating the hardware but it does not control the data nor does it exercise any editorial influence, other than running a complaints service. Information is organised by IPs (Information Providers), originally about 140 in number, all of which paid £4000 for the privilege plus £4 per frame per year. The minimum subscription is 100 pages, which were offered to the IPs on a first-come-first-served basis. Once obtained, the IPs have complete control over their pages and may use them themselves or rent them to other organisations or individuals. They must, however, take legal responsibility for all their pages and are required to indemnify British Telecom against any legal action arising from inaccurate or libellous contributions.

Information Providers work with a specific computer and revise their own pages through *editing ports,* which consist of a conventional VDU screen and keyboard plus special keys to govern block graphics and colour (seven colours are used in Prestel). A new page can be added in the following manner:

1. Generate new idea or obtain instructions from sub-contractor
2. Decide upon the number of frames
3. Design the frames
4. Structure new page into existing tree routes
5. Produce copy
6. Enter page into system
7. Proof read
8. Open it to user access
9. Maintain, correct and update it.

In many ways the IPs are publishers whilst British Telecom is the bookseller or newsagent, in so much as it provides the facilities to charge the customer while the IPs design the product. A bookseller, however, can decide not to stock certain magazines and can have many competing journals on the shelves. Whether Prestel will find certain information unacceptable remains to be seen. One area in which an attempt has been made to provide the user with more than one opinion is Consumer Advice but, again it is questionable whether a mere three statements constitute a comprehensive guide.

Closed user groups are another aspect of Prestel which have not yet been seriously considered. In the future organisations could have complete control of a number of pages, so much so that only their members would have access to them. Today stockbrokers run their own videotex system *Topic* which could easily be incorporated as a closed user group under Prestel and there is no reason why other institutions and organisations should not take advantage of such facilities. Individuals may even use Prestel to control their personal data handling requirements by incorporating a storage device, such as floppy discs, to hold a limited number of private pages locally.

Message communication is another facet of Prestel which is currently at an early stage of development. A user can store a message on the central computer which will then be transmitted to the recipient when they next access the system. The message must currently be one of a limited selection, such as 'Happy Birthday', but there is no reason why this *mailbox* feature should not evolve into an electronic mail service, where users construct their own messages. Opposition to this scheme may come from the conventional postal service, although their arguments will have diminished influence now that British Telecom has separated from the GPO.

3.5.2 Developments Overseas

Britain is not the only nation experimenting with a public videotex system, although it is currently the most advanced. France has a system called Teletel, Canada — Telidon and Vista, Finland — Teleset, Sweden — Datavision and Japan — Captain. In addition, West Germany, Holland and Switzerland have all purchased Prestel. It is interesting to compare the basic philosophies behind these different schemes for, although they are all videotex, there is considerable variance between the underlying structures. Prestel employs one of the many available approaches.

The Japanese system is the closest to Prestel, with an organised central computer network and no inter-subscriber communication. The main difference is the precision of the data display. Captain, from the beginning, had to cope with the 3500 or more Chinese and Japanese characters as well as the usual alphanumeric ones. To facilitate this they have developed a method by which signals are first coded by the computer and then decoded in the television set. A by-product of this character control is the excellent graphics available on Captain. One important feature of any microcomputer system is the sophistication of visual display. This is also true for videotex. Graphs, illustrations and photographic reproductions are as intrinsic a part of data communication as the typed word; British Telecom are launching a Picture Prestel in an attempt to improve their display.

Another system that considers clear graphics to be an essential element is the Canadian Telidon which, unlike Prestel, is distributed via cable TV rather than telephone lines. In Canada, over 80% of homes can be reached by cable TV and the advantage from the videotex point of view is in the increased amount of data that can be sent down this type of line compared with conventional telephone wires. To transmit clear TV pictures with sound, a large data transfer rate (or wide bandwidth) is required, whilst a sound only communication needs a small bandwidth. Therefore by using cable TV, Telidon can transmit data faster and hence build up in seconds complicated pictures which would take minutes of Prestel transmission. Fibre optics gives an enormous bandwidth, hence by tapping this potential, Telidon will give even clearer pictorial displays. A further distinction of the Canadian system is in the provision of a 'common video space'. This allows two subscribers to communicate with one another without having to go through a central computer. John Garrett (1980) considers that Telidon offers genuine 'community services' which set it apart from many other videotexes, such as the linking of automatic fire alarms to the local fire brigade.

The system which exhibits the most philosophical disparity from Prestel is the French Teletel. In this, the whole approach of the French authorities has been different, not least is the free provision of the necessary equipment to the users of the telephone system. By 1990 it hopes to have made available 30 million sets which, because of mass production could cost only £50 each. The immediate function of these sets will be as a directory enquiry service and paper directories, even local ones, will not be published in the future. This in itself will be a considerable saving in finance and paper. All national telephone enquiries will be made automatically through the household's terminal. This is bound to be an improvement on the somewhat unreliable system presently in operation in France. Having gained a guaranteed number of subscribers, i.e. the total telephone user population, Teletel can expand and progress from its initial, specific function.

Prestel provides the computer network and hires out pages to IPs; Teletel, on the other hand, operates with Service Providers who have their own computers as well as their own information. All the French PTT (equivalent of British Telecom) provides is a *packet switching* network which links all computers together and is available to all telephone subscribers. Teletel is a less centralised system than other videotexes and is therefore, not surprisingly, more flexible. One can contact Teletel without ever using any PTT equipment, by communicating directly with one of the computerised data bases. This suggests that a monopoly of national communications is not a prerequisite for a general information service.

Other proposed features of Teletel include the provision of a cheap facsimile printer to link to the free terminal and more sophisticated indexing. The printer will allow two or more users to transmit information directly, giving a similar service to Telidon, except that with the French system, written material and documents can be recreated at their destination — facsimile transfer. With indexing, one hopes to provide a keyword search facility so that any number of relevant pages can be 'thrown-up' when making a detailed examination of some aspect of the data library. Teletel and Prestel are so dissimilar in a number of vital areas, that an assessment of videotex *per se* is worthless. Each system must be considered in its own right if its full impact is to be analysed.

3.5.3 Viewdata is Newdata
Although British Telecom neither provides information itself nor exercises editorial control over those who do, the form in which Prestel has been organised and the priorities given to the various aspects of the system inevitably implies that ideological decisions have been and will continue to be taken by its management. These decisions, at the time economic or technical, will have a profound effect on many elements of our society especially if a viewdata information service seriously challenges traditional forms of data communication (as many people think it will). Hence it is of paramount importance that the consequences of introducing a new medium, such as videotex in general and Prestel in particular, be considered in detail before such systems become widespread, especially in educational establishments. As Rex Winsbury (1980) comments:

> ". . .viewdata's revolutionary potential lies precisely in it being the most concrete and most publicly visible example so far produced of the erosion of traditional demarcation lines and functions in the communications structure of society."

On the face of it, Prestel is a straightforward combination of a number of what society considers to be commonplace processes, namely the printed word, the television, the telephone, a large computer and a small hand-held control set. This simplistic view is misleading. Prestel, in common with all videotex systems has, by combining these media, produced something totally new to our society − a medium that will have its own scales of operation, constraints of use and underlying structural attitudes. One would expect such factors to arise from the internal conflicts implicit in the combination of such forms of communication.

The written or printed word is the orthodox form of communication used in books, newspapers and magazines, primarily controlled by private enterprise and consisting of a wide variety of contributions. Television, however, is a centralised, passive medium, concerned with visual entertainment and financed either by government money or advertising revenue. By comparison, the telephone is a participatory medium, decentralised in use but corporately owned and managed. Finally there are two types of computer, one contains large specifically structured data bases, the other is akin to a small calculator which, as a now commonplace tool, has its own connotations of speed, accuracy and correctness. It is not surprising that the end product of this combination is a medium with its very own identity; viewdata is a completely new information system and more than just an electronic version of an old one. As Marshall McLuhan (1964), the 1960s guru remarked:

". . . the personal and social consequences of any medium – that is, of any
extension of ourselves – result from the new scale that is introduced into our
affairs by each extension of ourselves, or by any new technology."

Earlier, a list was given of some of the more important properties associated
with the familiar form of communication, printed works. Similarly, Prestel may
be categorised into the following features:

1. An exclusive service available only to those with the necessary
   equipment.
2. Conflicting views and material are confined to a maximum of
   three statements to any one topic.
3. Initial hardware is expensive to purchase and there is a further
   charge on use.
4. Only a small percentage of Prestel service is allocated to regional
   information.
5. Size restriction: one frame has at most 880 characters, hence pages
   are limited.
6. Restricted indexing, allows only straightforward searching through
   the data library; browsing is difficult.
7. Prestel gives an unfamiliar mixture of news, official notices, advertising, encyclopedic knowledge and mail order.
8. The acquisition of information is quick with easy access by those
   with equipment.

Not all these characteristics are inherent in videotex; greater use will improve
familiarity and the development of more regional computers will give better
local coverage. In addition, France has shown that costs to the consumer can be
kept low and the indexing system made more flexible. Other restrictions remain,
however, such as the amount of data that can be displayed on the screen at one
time. The critical question is nevertheless that of access. The Post Office when
it first introduced the 'penny post' (see Chapter 2) substantially cut the cost of
the service and by doing so made it available to the whole population. Should
British Telecom adopt a similar approach to Prestel? Even if they go to the
French extreme and make the equipment free, not everybody has a telephone
or televeision or the inclination to use this type of equipment.

"The problem of people – perhaps only a small minority of people – who do not
have access to such systems . . . has already occurred in a different guise in the field
of transport where private cars have, in many areas, supplanted public transport,
it does not appear that solutions have been found to even this problem." (Stokes
1979).

The private car has led to a reduction in public transport, which affects those
members of the community who do not possess cars. If Prestel becomes the sole

supplier of even a small area of public knowledge then individuals without access to Prestel will be denied that knowledge.

Are Books and Newspapers Redundant?

Videotex is envisaged by many as being the major information supplier of the future with the printed page disappearing from common use. Certainly the current rising cost of production does indicate difficult times ahead for publishers whilst electronic systems, once operative, will run with low financial and resource requirements. But to assume that a decline in the circulation of newspapers and the sales of books can be paralleled by a surge in the use of Prestel is to grossly misunderstand the roles of the different media. Firstly, novels, which constitute a high proportion of all books, will never be an appropriate product for videotex, even in a future age where hand-held sets are in common use the aesthetic feel of a good book will remain. Before the personal receiver arrives, if it does at all, videotex will always suffer from a lack of mobility, one room in a house or one office in a corridor may have a Prestel terminal, but where do we usually spend our time reading? For myself, it is while I am travelling, for others it is in bed or in quiet contemplation, and how can I get New Scientist, Nursing Times and The Beano at the same time? Prestel will quite evidently not change our natural reading habits.

Due to its many structural constraints, Prestel's most significant shortcoming is that it fails to present any kind of in-depth analysis as its content has to be terse. This is acceptable when dealing with the Financial Times Index, Test Match scorecard or British Rail timetable as these *facts* are well understood in such brevity. Many other items of information, analysis or news can only be described within the social and political framework in which they exist. Encyclopedias have not replaced the more detailed specialist book, nor has television news superseded the morning newspaper, for they cannot give the same coverage. Consider a random statistical sample of one edition of the Guardian newspaper. A quick calculation − without the aid of a pocket calculator − gives a Prestel equivalent of 1200 frames! One newspaper, however, is insufficient, peoples opinions and attitudes favour six or seven daily papers as well as a host of evening editions and the weekly magazines.

It is inconceivable that Prestel could accomodate this volume of material daily, the best it could possibly achieve is a short coverage of the headlines, which is far removed from being a news service. Although Fleet Street is experiencing problems associated with microelectronics it will have nothing to fear from videotex for many years, for Prestel as a new information medium will complement existing forms but should not be allowed to replace them.

3.5.4 The Right of Reply

After the protection of one's own privacy and the right of access to public knowledge, there is a third element of what is often called the democratic rights of an individual in an information society, namely, to participate, to voice one's own opinions and ideas, rather than being a mere passive consumer of information. In Britain, unlike the United States for example, there is a tradition of prohibiting individuals and organisations from being the instigators of any type of broadcast. Witness the debate over Citizens Band Radio which only now, after considerable pressure and mounting uncontrolled abuse, is to be legalised. With Prestel the philosophy has similarly been one of restricting the participatory part of the system. Information is provided by a small group of professionals, licenced to give knowledge to the people. The pages are stored only on official computers run by British Telecom, who then allows access to the public. Such a system is rigid and hierarchical.

Roger Haines and John Garrett of the *Information 2000* pressure group consider there to be no implicit reason why videotex should be so hierarchical. They feel that by encouraging our participation, interaction and side-ways communication even Prestel could be made to resemble more of a lateral democratic information service.

> "Viewdata is meant to be interactive, a system whereby the traditional difference between publisher and reader, broadcaster and receiver, originator and user is abolished. There may be only a transitory phase during which those distinctions again inherited from elsewhere are kept up. Thereafter the ability of *anyone* (his italics) to communicate two-way with the viewdata computer may become the dominant characteristic in its use." (Winsbury 1980).

In attempting to assess the likely impact of the widespread use of videotex, one must return to the questions asked at the beginning of this chapter. What objectives is it meant to serve? How successful is it in fulfilling objectives? Who controls its use? What skills are required by its users? What are the psychological problems associated with its application? How will the new technology interact with society as a whole? We have considered in detail one example of the new information services, Prestel. Other schemes, such as the one envisaged in France, would furnish different responses to the questions above. If Prestel is to be a truly public system it will need to evolve along the right lines for confidence and popular use to ensue. Some of the features listed below would, if encouraged, go a long way towards this:

1. Provide cheap and easy access – public Prestel stations in libraries, community centres etc.
2. Make the Information Providers more accesible and accountable.
3. Provide local data areas so that a 'community noticeboard' can be built up, in which users can participate.
4. Establish 'mailbox' facilities for communication of messages between users. (Protection against unsolicited advertising would need to be coupled with this).

5. Offer scope for direct communication between two or more users.
6. Give provision for users to hold their own pages on suitable storage equipment, for personal use and that of small organisations. (This would, in effect, break the British Telecom monopoly of control of all the systems' data bases).
7. Include the development of a suitable indexing system, with particular reference to (6) so that the whole system does not become unwieldy.

3.6 EDUCATION AND TRAINING

In a rapidly changing society, where traditional skills and knowledge can become redundant virtually overnight, it is imperative that we make our training and educational systems as efficient as possible. It has become customary to blame education for the evils of our contemporary society whilst at the same time expecting it to resolve all future problems. Schools are required to produce the right number of qualified personnel to run the new technology as well as prepare the rest of the population to fit into the changing social orders brought about by its use. Moreover, schools are expected to accomplish this with no improvement in teacher training, little opportunity for in-service secondments and against a background of general financial constraint. There may have been a time in the distant past when a period of training at an early age would have equipped one for life. This is no longer the case, information affecting our work, pastimes and environment is constantly bombarding us, from the time we leave school or college until long after our retirement. Education is therefore, be it formally recognised or not, a life long activity. Initially our employment is most affected by changing social orders and this has a number of educational consequences; knowledge is no longer the sole province of 'the elders':

"If I had a son in the business (Engineering) I would have no traditional wisdom, no craft skill, nothing of relevance to import to him − a point of some social significance." (Laver 1974).

Then there is the more drastic problem of having to face the fact that one's trade and particular work experience may not be a passport to permanent work, even in a time of economic boom. For many people this will be difficult to come to terms with, but in the future it may become the norm to retrain and change careers two or three times during one's working life, rather than expect job training at the age of sixteen or twenty-one to be still relevant forty years later.

Before discussing actual teaching schemes, it is worth emphasising that education and training are not the same thing. Education takes place over a fairly long time, during which students assimilate a variety of concepts, facts, techniques and methods of working associated with a particular range of topics. Training, on the other hand, is more the acquisition of specific skills of a band of knowledge, usually on top of a more general education and taking place over a relatively short period of time. It is not the role of this book to consider the nature of education, but the description and assessment of any technology would not be complete if it did not include reference to the skills and knowledge that the technology requires from, or can give to, society as a whole. One critical aspect of any analysis of technology is the degree to which it uses indigenous skills, and the level to which its design and function are generally understood.

As well as the training aspect of technology there is also the technical aspect of education to consider. Information technology is being used increasingly in schools and colleges to help in the teaching process. This raises a number of questions as to the appropriateness of various CAI and CAL (Computer Assisted Instruction and Computer Aided Learning) schemes. What objectives are such schemes meant to serve? How successful are they in fulfilling these objectives? And what, if any, are the psychological problems associated with such techniques? In simple terms, technological advancement needs committed educational training support which, in turn use elements of the technology to accomplish this task. It is evident that the two are interelated, society therefore must make every effort to structure education correctly, as this may well be the only real control that it has over the technology.

3.6.1 Post-School Training

Until recently, the only way of 'getting into' computers was to undertake a period of education in a university or polytechnic or, alternatively, to obtain experience by working for a large firm which uses computers and then, if one felt the need, acquire one of the many BCS (British Computer Society) qualifications. As one would expect from a three year university course, the aim is to give a very broad grounding in all aspects of computing and, perhaps, to link this with one of the more traditional subjects such as mathematics or physics. Only in the last few years has 'computer science' became a subject in its own right. The curricula for undergraduate courses in computer science at British universities are similar to those across the world and were, at least initially, based on a formula published by the American Computer Society in 1968 (ACM 1968). At one time it was difficult to fill three years study with relevant material, now one can barely cover all the elements of the science in this time. Topics include: basic hardware structure, chip design, micro, mini and mainframe computer systems, networks, high level languages (Ada, Pascal, COBOL and others), all areas of application, operating systems, artificial intelligence, expert systems, informatics, real time systems, systems analysis etc. There are now undergraduate courses that specialise in particular areas of computing such as data processing or microtechnology.

The relevance of microelectronics in our society is well illustrated by the popularity of these university and college courses, but to qualify for such a course a high educational standard is required. When computer users had to understand the internal workings of the machine, it was obvious that only electrical engineers would be able to operate them. As programming developed, more people became involved with computers but whilst low-level languages were the norm it was still the specialist who dealt with them. Today things are different, it is no longer necessary to have a degree to work with computers. Operators, programmers (in high-level languages), analysts and data processing personnel constitute the bulk of the people working in the computing field and these jobs are available to most. Since it has been estimated that there is a current shortage of over 20,000 programmers in Britain, how does one become trained in the new skills?

Due to the apparent sophistication of anything to do with computers or microelectronics, it has previously been very difficult to find any relevant course, unless you wished and were able to go to university or would pay for one of the many privately organised, expensive training schemes. The situation is now somewhat easier, with a number of training programmes being available. The TOPS programme has been placing suitable candidates for more six years, most students obtain some form of qualification at the end of the course (for example, most trainee programmers take City and Guilds exams). But it is the experience gained by students which is of attraction to prospective employers.

The NCC Threshold Scheme
Whilst TOPS aims primarily at persons wishing to change career direction, for the young employed there is a different scheme run jointly by the NCC (National Computing Centre) and the MSC (Manpower Services Commission). This is a newer type of course, in which the students are financed by the MSC, and again it appears to be very successful. The NCC organises the material and content of the training but invites local colleges to run them, they last for twenty-four weeks of which eight are spent on industrial placement. There are two types of course offered under this scheme which run in parallel. One is solely concerned with programming while the other deals with a combination of programming and operation. The industrial placement element has a number of uses. Not only does it furnish the student with valuable experience but it also helps employers to appreciate that useful skills and abilities can be acquired after only a short period of training.

In the absence of an NCC scheme, local organisations, such as those in Leeds and London, have set up 'Technology Projects' to train people in elements of the new industry. Courses last about six months and concentrate on programming, microcomputers or computer operations, using bench electronic equipment. Being community-based projects, the emphasis is usually placed on local needs, with 'general awareness' classes given and 'useful' tools built. Alarms for the elderly and aids for the handicapped are examples of the micro-based devices that have been constructed after less than half a year's training. This type of project attempts to add an element of education to the training programme to hopefully instil in students an appreciation of the role of computer technology.

> "But even as the growth of research and teaching related to data processing expands to meet the needs, first expressed a decade earlier, there is a growing realisation that the education basis chosen is still too narrow. We have been training computer professionals whose outlook is biased towards the machine." (Land 1979).

Training is becoming more available and the success of the present schemes have helped dissipate the mystique surrounding microelectronics and computers. Specialists will always require extensive training no matter what their field, but the speed at which people have come to be familiar with, and effectively use, computers is a valuable pointer to future trends.

3.6.2 School Education
For too many people, education begins and ends with school. It is imperative, therefore, that an awareness of modern technology be given in these institutions. In 1978 over 21,000 pupils took examinations in computer science, compared with only a handful in 1970, and the number is growing every year. Formal examinations in CSE and GCE are, in many ways, a poor indication of the actual teaching taking place in the classroom, but they do illustrate that schools are encompassing, what many people would consider to be, highly pertinent subject matter in their curriculae.

The Four R's (Reading, wRiting, aRithmetic and pRogramming)
After considerable pressure from various educationalists, the Department of Education and Science announced early in 1980 that it was making £9 million available to schools and colleges, over a four year period, to help bring micro-electronics into the classroom (the original plan was for £12.5 million over five years). Equipment is obviously required, as each school should have micro-computers, but equally important is the training of the teachers who will have the responsibility of running the computing courses. Some areas, such as London, have decided to establish special centres with full-time staff who can tour the local schools giving detailed advice. Other parts of the country are less fortunate and it is left to the odd enthusiastic teacher to supervise perhaps one thousand pupils on two or three microcomputers.

Organisations such as TEACH (Technology Education And Change) have, for some time, monitored the use of microcomputers in schools, with the journal *Educational Computing* becoming a forum for much reflection and debate. TEACH have formulated a list of priorities, which they wish to see put into action. They include:

1. Courses, conferences, seminars and awareness programmes for teacher trainers.
2. The incorporation of microelectronic issues in all teacher training.
3. Massive provision of in-service courses for teachers of all disciplines.
4. Special courses for teachers of microelectronics.
5. Setting up of support networks.
6. A massive expansion in training provisions for teachers who will be needed in continuing education and re-training programmes.

If society is going to obtain the skills required to adequately control and use microelectronic technology, what subjects should the school student be studying?

First, a general familiarity with standard equipment must be acquired, this can probably be facilitated through using such equipment in other subjects as teaching aids. One straightforward skill easily taught by practice in a number of teaching situations is keyboard literacy. So many examples of modern technology involve a keyboard that it is reasonable to expect school leavers to have developed some expertise in typing. As has been emphasised in this book, technology itself cannot be effectively examined without considering its application and therefore detailed courses on computers must encompass the dual issues of understanding *how* and *why* technology functions as it does. The history of computing and microelectronics is as good a framework as any on which to structure such material.

There remains one further important skill which should be included in all school curriculae, programming. Programming is the passport to understanding and using micros and may in the future rival reading, writing and arithmetic as essential training for the modern society. Perhaps pRogramming could even become one of the *four* fundamental Rs. As well as being a useful skill, it introduces students to a number of abstract concepts which would be of value in themselves, constituting as they do one further facet of an overall thinking mode.

There are, however, dangers in developing 'compthink' which should also be recognised. Not all problems are amenable to computer solution, so a distinction must be drawn between work suitable for computers and that which is not. Also the discrete nature of computer languages and the symbolic form they take, makes it obvious that only measurable quantities can be included in computer analysis, whereas in reality most problems have elements that, though crucial, are not quantifiable. The 'never mind what is important, what can you measure' syndrome must be recognised and counteracted in any educational programme.

In the final analysis, the teaching of microelectronics, computer awareness and programming in schools is dependent upon the availability of funds. The British Government has contributed £9 million which, in terms of the cost of a microcomputer is a lot of money, but does not appear quite so generous when measured against expenditure on teacher training and re-training. Education is expected to adapt to future trends but is never given sufficient funding. Many schools, short of books and staff, organise fund raising events in order to buy a microcomputer. If the demise of the book and the newspaper is to be a feature of a post-industrial society then we appear to be making a good start in our schools.

Other nations are tackling the problems of computer education in an entirely different light, the French for example aim to have substantial computing facilities in all their schools by 1990, and will put *informatique* at the centre of their educational system.

Drills and Practice

This section has so far been concerned with the acquistion of skills in micro-electronics and computers. The more people who can understand and hence use the technology the less chance there is of it unwittingly disturbing existing social and environmental orders. Within education, however, there is the more specific question of how to assess technological aids for use in the actual teaching process.

> "No aspect of human life is likely to remain wholly unaffected by this remarkable development (microelectronics), least of all education, by its nature preoccupied with the very business of storing, retrieving and disseminating information." (Gosling 1978).

It is clear that information technology has a role to play in education. One of the earliest techniques to have emerged is where the computer provides *drill and practice*. With this method the computer is programmed to display, on a VDU, a series of simple questions to which the student must reply. Their responses are analysed and appropriate messages are returned. Correct answers are affirmed and incorrect replies given a hint as to the acceptable solution, the student normally being given three attempts before being told what the correct answer is. Quite sophisticated programs can be developed on this theme; for example a drill and practice arithmetic test might recognise that a student has most trouble with three digit mulitplication and would therefore provide more of this type of question; another user may be given more division problems to solve. Probably the most popular examples of drill and practice aids are those which test spelling; modern hand-held devices even have a voice synthesiser to pronounce the word to be spelt. Other systems test translation from one language to another; for example, one can be obtained which will act as a French-English dictionary as well as a French tester.

It is important to realise that drill and practice machines do not teach students but rather test them; they can be used to consolidate ideas but cannot introduce new concepts. Even as testers their use is limited because not all sub-jects fall into a simple question and answer formulation, it might be appropriate for arithmetic but not for general problem solving. There is an increasing trend in education, especially in the United States, for computers to be used for formal examination and marking in all manner of subjects. The attraction of this method is that the computer is both unbiased and accurate, and in purely objective disciplines there may be something to be gained from these methods. In other areas objectivity is not possible, or more precisely should not be made possible, as the material itself is subjective. Essay type questions test more than just factual knowledge, they illustrate an ability to balance, order and communicate information, an activity that would be very difficult to examine by drill and practice.

CAI and CAL

Computer Assisted Instruction and Computer Aided Learning have gone beyond simple drill and practice; they constitute actual teaching machines. The computer takes on the role of tutor, introducing material, answering questions and testing the student's understanding of the topics just covered. The software for CAI is considerably more complicated than that of a simple tester and hence it takes somewhat longer to develop. One of the earliest large education systems to meet this challenge was MECC (Minnesota Education Computing Consortium) which was responsible for all computer equipment in Minnesota schools. In 1976 MECC opened what was, at the time, the world's largest timesharing computer system. It was based on two Univac machines and was capable of dealing with 440 terminals (VDUs) at once, that is it could control unique teaching sequences for 440 students simultaneously.

Another famous educational teaching system is PLATO which runs on a CDC machine for the Illinois area. Project students from junior grade up to college level sit at VDUs and are taken by the computer through a teaching session on one of a large number of possible subjects. 'Real live' teachers are available to answer questions but the students are encouraged to ask the computer first; the software is very good at recognising the meaning of typed sentences, even if they are grammatically incorrect. Rewards, such as allowing the user to play one of the many games on the system, are readily used in the teaching method.

Considerable success has been attributed to these projects and their valuable use in training is beyond doubt. In education the benefits are not as easy to ascertain for it depends upon the overall objectives. One important role of school education must be to develop communication skills and social training, to help pupils live, work and converse with other members of the community. It is questionable whether CAI and CAL can satisfy these needs; in the United States, children have been observed to become almost addicted to the computer, an introverted child would much rather play with the machine than with other children. Incidentally, these 'computerholics' are by no means restricted to school children; many university students and other adult computer users seem to have a predilection for sitting with their eyes only a foot away from a VDU for long periods of time. In many schools it may be necessary to restrict the amount of time any pupil can have under CAI, a situation that should please the teachers who in the long term fear they might find themselves partly replaced by such machines.

Behind Marshall McLuhan's phrase 'The Medium is the Message', lies the belief that in any process of learning, what we actually experience is not what is being taught but how it is being done; what comes across is knowledge of the medium rather than its content. This implies that what we learn from books is totally different from that derived via television, radio, lecture or film, even if the subject matter is the same. If this is indeed the case then the consequences of replacing a human teacher with an attentive VDU link is far from clear, and it would be particularly significant to know:

(a) Do pupils obey computer commands more readily than human ones?
(b) Are pupils more likely to 'believe' a computer than a human?
(c) Are children's attitudes to computer technology affected by initially encountering it as a machine-tutor?
(d) Does computer usage help structure knowledge in an appropriate way?

If the overall impact of educational technology is to be predicted then attention must be paid to these questions. In some circumstances, children may find computers more credible than humans and look solely to them as providers of accurate information. This trend may be regarded as being of positive benefit by some educationalists, others may think it an area of conern as it could lead to indiscriminate use of the technology after the children have left school.

Simulation Packages

One type of CAL package is used to simulate elements of everyday life with as realistic a basis as possible. The user is normally allowed to alter certain parameters of the simulation and the computer then presents them with predictions on the likely effects of their actions. Many mathematical and physical problems can be represented in this manner and the student can obtain a true 'feel' of the system being simulated through the ability to change whatever variables he or she wishes.

This technique is not only of use in education; for many engineering problems this is the only way in which likely behaviour can be anticipated. The reason for this is either due to the cost of building an actual experimental rig or because the features under consideration are too difficult or dangerous to obtain in real life; simulations of nuclear power stations are popular for testing potentially disasterous problems. Similarly, nuclear attack can be simulated on large computers to test national defences although, as we have seen, these programs can occasionally be taken for the real thing: which could lead to the possibility of a self-fulfilling simulation.

On a more mundane level, software packages have been developed that can simulate the thermal behaviour of a house under varying weather conditions. The program user can decide on such factors as the type of insulation the house might have, whether or not it is double glazed, how it is heated and to what temperature, the use of solar panels and the existence of a heat store. The simulation then portrays seasonal behaviour and calcualtes the cost of keeping the house at the required temperature, by comparing the fuel saving with the capital cost, and the breakthrough time (the payback time for the initial expense).

Another example of a simulation package models fishing stocks in a 'typical' ocean. The user is allowed to catch any variety of fish to whatever level desired, and the simulator will then calculate the effect on fishing stocks. After many attempts and frequent annihilation of the total fish population, it becomes obvious that there is a maximum catch level over which it is counter-productive to fish (a program with a moral!). Users of these packages can quickly grasp the problem and over the course of a number of runs acquire considerable working knowledge, otherwise difficult to obtain. There are many other simulation programs of this sort but full-time teachers seldom have the time to construct them, with the result that these valuable educational aids are only gradually becoming available.

With simulation software, there is still the question of the extent to which students are influenced by their use. The main advantage of this type of study is that experience can be gained on models that would not otherwise be possible. The disadvantages stem from the potential misconceptions introduced during a simulation; no model, no matter how well constructed, can replace reality. Whether it is appropriate to ignore this distinction when using teaching aids remains to be seen.

4

The Appropriate use of Micro-electronics

"No one has yet projected a society in which the computer serves to enhance individuality or to make possible a genuine participatory democracy." (Mowshowitz 1977).

There are many instances where microelectronic technology has been applied inappropriately, where neither the user nor the general community have benefitted by its deployment. One may argue whether this is an inherent fault in the technology itself or rather, as many technologists believe, the inability of society to regulate its own affairs. Designers may wish to abdicate responsibility for the outcome of their work, but should they be allowed to enjoy economic and social neutrality? The microprocessor itself, being by nature a raw material, may indeed be a neutral device but the design of the systems and equipment that incorporate it are not; they must reflect the influences, prejudices and motivations of those who control their manufacture and use. Changes in the pattern of work reflect the market economy; information and educational systems are affected by the properties and scale of the medium employed, and personal surveillance and privacy violations mirror the political climate.

By looking at the ways in which microelectronics have already been applied and by trying to evaluate their effectiveness and impact, one can learn from past mistakes and predict where these may recur unless further planning, analysis or legislation can curtail possible social disharmonies. It is significant that although computerised systems appear to be designed to promote efficiency and financial success, their deployment must be a contentious issue. This antagonism must surely be due to the criteria around which the technology is structured. If computerised systems could be developed under different objectives then perhaps their application would become more unilaterally beneficial or acceptable.

The large computers found in major companies and institutions have led to greater centralisation and bureaucracy, but the distinguishing feature of the micro is that it dispenses with the need for such concentration of resources. Although microprocessors have only been on the market a relatively short time, there are already more microcomputers in use by individuals and small organisations than by large institutions, and the devolution of many extensive data processing systems has commenced. Applied correctly, microelectronics can accelerate the tendency towards decentralisation and a more personalised society. The condensed size, robust nature and low cost of a microcomputer helps it become more accessible to all and easily used for a variety of tasks in a number of different locations. Computers no longer need specially trained staff and purpose built air-conditioned rooms.

The Convivial Chip
Unlike the bulky mainframe computers, the compactness of the microprocessor will help a move toward smaller units. It would be well however to consider whether its advantages are confined to physical suitability or extend to other potential and more abstract benefits. Microcomputers are rarely ends in themselves, they are merely tools and therefore computer specialists are toolsmiths. But do they constitute what Ivan Illich (1973) deems 'a convivial tool'? and can microelectronics be described as an appropriate technology? The features associated with such a technology were dealt with in detail in Chapter 1; the following is a summary:

1. Intelligible to the community.
2. Accessible to all.
3. Fulfil social need.
4. Locally controlled.
5. Use indigenous skills and resources.
6. No job loss.
7. No user health hazards.
8. Non-pollutant.
9. Provides fulfilling, flexible, creative and innovative usage.
10. Prevents external cultural domination.
11. Does not disturb existing social order.

If one now applied an assessment similar to that outlined in the previous chapter one would find that appropriate technologies are those that are easily understood, readily available, use attainable skills and resources in their manufacture and use, are safe to apply, are of overall social benefit and can interact with elements of society without undue disturbance.

How well does microelectronics fit this description? In terms of job loss we saw in the last chapter that this is an open-ended question, though in the short term the position looks bleak. If we are truly moving towards a post-industrial society, it may be proper to remove point (6) from the above list, since it will no longer be important; but to do that now would be an insult to the millions unemployed in Europe alone. Of the many elements which make up an appropriate technology, the most significant must be that it fulfils some social goal, so consideration of actual applications which fall into this category will be discussed in the next chapter. As for the other features which constitute conviviality, they will be dealt with by reference to the following four questions about microelectronics:

(a) What is the social and environmental cost of production of the microelectronic raw material, the chip?

(b) What are the social and environmental consequences of the application of microelectronic based equipment?

(c) What elements of user design and control can there be over such equipment?

and

(d) To what extent will microbased equipment help the user express *creativity* and *vision* when undertaking a *flexible* range of tasks?

4.1 THE SOCIAL AND ENVIRONMENTAL COST OF PRODUCTION

In Chapter 2 the mechanism by which microprocessors are produced was described in terms of four basic stages; research and development, fabrication, assembly and testing. Each stage requires special personnel and machinery, the costs of which may be viewed in terms of their use of natural resources and their demands upon the workforce. As one would expect, the research and development work is undertaken by specialists who design the multi-layered circuits and prepare large circuit drawings which are then photographically reduced to produce the mask for the chip. Computer aided design tools are invariably employed to alleviate the tedious aspects of drawing these diagrams which, as the all-important blueprint for production, furnish their creators with considerable remuneration.

The next stage is the capital intensive manufacture in which each layer of silicon is first doped with impurities, then etched with the circuit design and finally baked in purpose built ovens. Once all the layers have been built up, the complete wafer of chips is tested on elaborate equipment and the defective products marked. The ratio of worthless to working chips can be as high as 9:1. Due to the high cost of machinery manufacturing is usually situated close to company headquarters. Initially these were all situated in California's 'Silicon Valley' but since then semiconductor firms have sprung up in many areas of the developed world, not only in Japan but also in Wales and in Scotland, where the production of specialised chips has led to the use of the phrase 'Silicon Glen'.

Because this part of the operation has taken place chiefly in industrial nations the working conditions of the employees are of an acceptable standard even though dangerous chemicals are used in many aspects of production. The factories are spotlessly clean – the manufacturing process demands it – and use tolerably low levels of energy and natural resources. Silicon is sand, and the second commonest element on our planet and hence there is no question of using up a rare natural resource, even with a 90% failure rate. The machines that make micros are themselves instruments of high technology and can be considered as examples of very sophisticated photographic equipment, working on a small scale to produce a large number of items at low cost. Unlike the highly technical manufacturing stage, assembly is very labour-intensive as it involves cutting the wafers into individual chips, discarding the duds and then *bonding* the working chips. They have up to fifty minute wires attached with the result that the assembly worker has to be constantly looking through a microscope. Once bonded, each chip is sealed in a plastic or ceramic coating for protection. The extremely high cost of research and development coupled to low profit margins and a continuing expectation of a high growth rate has resulted in the semiconductor companies being very conscious of their labour costs. Even though many chip components are in short supply, the pressure to produce cheaper and more extensive microprocessors has put many semiconductor firms out of business and applied increased pressure on the remaining multinational companies.

Attempts to minimise labour costs are primarily centred round the assembly process; initially this work was undertaken by women in California (because of lower wages) but as with other areas of electronics, the attraction of a low wage expectancy precipitated developments in the third world. Initially it was to Mexico then to the even cheaper labour markets of Asia with Fairchild setting up the first Asian assembly plant at Hong Kong in 1962. The electronics/semiconductor industry has since moved progressively through Southeast Asia: Singapore in 1969, Malaysia in 1972, Thailand in 1973 and Indonesia and the Philipines in 1974 (SAC 1979). The reasons for these moves were aptly explained by a manager in Malaysia:

"One worker working one hour produces enough to pay the wages of ten workers working one shift plus all the costs of materials and transport."

Altogether between 200,000 and 300,000 women work in electronics factories throughout Southeast Asia, over eighteen of these factories being situated on the one island of Penang, Malaysia including an Intel plant employing over 1400 assembly workers, where 90% of them are women.

A cursory look at these industries might give the impression that the actions of the semiconductor companies are quite acceptable, even laudable. They bring capital, work and technology to the developing world, the factories appear clean and cheerful, the wages are reasonable by local standards, the workforce is well looked after and opportunities are given for women to work in their own right, releasing them from their traditional second class roles. Unfortunately, a more detailed examination raises a number of alarming factors. Rachael Crossman (presently a member of the Southeast Asia Resource Group) has travelled extensively through Southeast Asia and reported at length on the effects of building high technology factories in rural Asia. In a detailed analysis of the situation in Malaysia (Crossman 1979), a number of disturbing implications are highlighted and she is not alone in drawing attention to the foundation on which the modern electronic economy of the developed world is based. (Lim 1978, Chen 1978, AMPO 1977, PSC 1977).

Employment

Undoubtedly one of the main attractions of a large electronics factory from a Southeast Asian Government's point of view, is the prospect of a significant reduction in the local, usually high, unemployment; after all, a single factory can employ over one and a half thousand assembly workers. Unfortunately, the electronics industry requires young, educated workers (high school) with a decided preference given to female labour. Rather than reduce unemployment they have created a new category of worker. L.Y.C.Lim found that, in Penang, over two thirds of the workforce were in their first job and, moreover, they came from families in which the female members had never previously worked for wages.

The Malaysian Government considers only men when defining the 'actively unemployed', the 19,000 female workers on the island of Penang have done little to help this figure. On the contrary, when assembly lines are closed down they are in a much worse situation than when they started, for it is difficult for women to return from the factories to their families to reassume a traditional role; their income has become a necessity upon which their families have come to depend.

Wages

The average assembly worker is usually young, female and single, three catogeries that universally imply comparatively low wages. In Malaysia after two years experience a worker would probably be earning the equivalent of 100 US dollars a month. To give some indication of the value of this amount, her basic expenditure would be $45, for rent (bed or floor in a shared room), food and transport. When she began work however she would probably only be earning $54-$60, which would barely cover her necessities. In addition she would be expected to send home between a quarter and a half of her income to help keep her family. This low starting wage can continue for up to six months even though most of the 'skills of the trade' can be learnt in one or two weeks. In Indonesia and the Philippines, the position is considerably worse with many cases of the starting wage being below not only the necessity level but also the legal minimum.

The Factory Subculture

Probably the most disquieting feature of situating a modern factory in a traditionally rural community is the unusual life style it imposes on the work force. A high proportion of the women workers are immigrant and come from neighbouring towns and states in order to find jobs. They are therefore estranged from their families; an uncommon situation in these communities. Most of the women live in shared rooms close to the factories, many are even chaperoned at the request of their fathers. To enable inexperienced workers to adjust to the regimented work schedules and shift systems, companies organise a variety of fringe activities including beauty contests, fashion shows and make-up demonstrations to help bond the work force. They consider themselves as parental figures. One manager of a Fairchild plant in Indonesia explained it thus:

> "What we are doing resembles a family system in which I am not just the manager but also a father to all of those here at Fairchild."

These organised recreations together with a full working day (an eight hour shift with perhaps only one forty-five minute break) result in the women's total existance being structured around the company. Performance pressure is considerable, productivity levels must be maintained and each women risks being laid off should she fail to fulfill her own particular quota. The women, in effect, live in a sub-culture totally divorced from the general community to which they must inevitably return once they no longer work for the company.

Health and Safety
Although a superficially clean and pleasant working environment exists in all electronics factories where the employers encourage increased safety standards with warning posters, essay contests, fire drills and an annual health and safety week, there remain a number of work practices which would not be tolerated in factories in the developed world. The testing of chips before they are bonded requires constant use of a microscope. A woman in an optical test station would spend perhaps seven hours a day peering through a lens and be expected to test around 3,500 chips per shift. Rachael Crossman reports that:

> "After three or four years a worker's vision begins to blur so that she can no longer meet the production quotas."

Virtually everyone who stays at this job for over three years wears glasses permanently.

If one's job is bonding, there are other hazards to face, caustic and toxic chemicals are used throughout the process:

> "Workers who must dip components in acids and rub them with solvents frequently experience serious burns, dizziness, nausea, sometimes even losing their fingers in accidents. A major cause of accidents is the high speed at which workers are required to carry out their tasks. It will be ten or fifteen years before the possible carcinogenic effects of these chemicals begin to show up in the women who work with them now." (SAC 1979)

Clearly the electronic assembly lines are far from reaching the kind of standards laid down in, say, the British Health and Safety at Work Act.

Government Policy

It would be wrong to give the impression that the large multinational semi-conductor companies are in any sense forcing their way into Southeast Asia. On the contrary, governments looking for development capital have welcomed the fast moving, highly technical electronic organisations. They have gone to considerable pains to point out the advantages of their own particular setting and the availability of pools of cheap female labour. For example, a Malaysian brochure, 'The Solid State For Electronics', contains the following statement:

> "The manual dexterity of the oriental female is famous the world over. Her hands are small and she works fast with extreme care. Who, therefore, could be better qualified by nature and inheritance to contribute to the efficiency of a bench-assembly production line than the oriental girl?"

Other actions taken to encourage overseas investment have included the relaxation of laws prohibiting night work for women and the declaration that foreign-owned manufacturing plants are 'vital' — it is illegal to strike in a vital industry. Trade Unions are not welcomed by electronic firms, neither in the developing nor the developed world!

Future Prospects

Governments that have encouraged companies to set up assembly lines in their countries in order to share in the electronics boom have, on the whole, been disappointed with the outcome. Revenue may indeed have been generated but the expected reductions in unemployments levels have not materialised, mainly due to the type of worker the semiconductor companies require. There is also the inescapable evidence that electronics manufactures can never be considered a permanent feature in any particular area. Competition has caused many bankruptcies and even the successful companies are always looking for cheaper labour markets, witness the move across Southeast Asia. During the 1974 recession one third of all electronics workers in Singapore lost their jobs. The result of such uncertainties is that developing nations can niether plan long term strategies nor depend on the creation of a thriving infrastructure around electronics. For the work force the future is equally precarious, even if the factories remain, they themselves can only work for perhaps a maximum of four to five years. In that time they will have become accustomed to living a company life-style and earning a regular income. Many families will have become completely dependent upon this money for, with high unemployment, a woman is often the sole wage earner in a wide family circle. After leaving work, it may become impossible for the women to return to their previous way of life and yet the skills they have learnt on the assembly line are totally inappropriate for any alternative work that might be available in a developing community. Many women have no option but to move to the cities and live as best they can.

4.1.1 The Global Assembly Line

Because microelectronic devices are small and light, it is economically sensible to ship them half way across the world where they can be assembled by the cheapest labour possible. Once assembled the chips have to be finally tested. This takes place in California or Japan, although an increasing number of testing sites are being set up in some of the more developed areas of Asia, such as Hong Kong and South Korea. Having passed inspection, the chip could be shipped back to the US or Europe and sold as a bare microprocessor or used in some specialist equipment. Alternatively, if the chip is to be incorporated into a mass sales product it would more probably be forwarded to another area of Asia, ending up as the power behind a pocket calculator or as one element of a computer circuit board. Eventually, all such products are returned to the developed world for either direct sale or the final stage of assembly.

It is this last part that makes the exploitation of the Asian cultures so deplorable; not only are the production skills unnatural and worthless in a developing nation, but the end product itself is of no value or use locally. Personal computers, control apparatus and telecommunication equipment are elements of high technology destined for the rich parts of the globe and they have no role to play in the Third World. Later we will consider whether the micro has any appropriate uses in Britain (or Europe and the USA) and examples of socially and environmentally motivated applications will be given. But this is only within the context of the Northern nations,[†] in the South the micro is a luxury. Technologies here are required that will provide greater employment, encourage the uptake of simple, useful skills and furnish worthwhile products needed locally as well as abroad.

The predicament faced by the Southeast Asian people is that if they attempt to raise wage rates in the semiconductor industries, then these industries will simply move elsewhere, leaving the local economy in a worse position than before. When there is no cheap labour left anywhere, it will be profitable to invest in more automated plants. Already there is a move back to California and Japan with the advent of capital intensive, labour scarce assembly lines. If the assembly line process is an inherent health hazard then it is only right that micro-based robots be used to produce more micros. Moreover, if these chip based products are only used in developed countries then they should be manufactured entirely in these countries so that their price justifiably reflects the full economic cost of their production.

When or if the post-industrial society arrives, it will depend heavily upon sophisticated electronics, just as the industrial society is based on fuel and energy. We have recently observed the effects of oil shortages and price rises which emphasise the fact that, for too long, oil has been sold at an unrealistically

[†] The latest terminology to be used in the labelling of rich and poor nations has been given by Willy Brandt and his commission on International Development.

low price. If the micro is the raw material of tomorrow's society, then we must ensure that its production has no detrimental social or economic consequences. Environmentally, microelectronics is a clean technology and if costs remain reasonable, it should become increasingly available to all members of our society. The argument as to whether robots or Asian women should assemble micros will have little effect on the march of the micro but for the Third World, there is a world of difference.

4.2 THE SOCIAL AND ENVIRONMENTAL COST OF USAGE
Two of the most important characteristics of any technology are that they should be both non-pollutant and energy efficient. The modern microcomputer uses virtually no power at all. Because the logic components on the chip are so densely packed, very little energy is required to move 'information' around. As chips become more compact and hence sophisticated, their energy needs will diminish. The low power requirement of the microcomputer is in stark contrast to the extravagant amounts of electricity used by the older larger computers. The difference is due to two effects; a large computer, not built of LSI technology, needs a lot of electricity to run and, in addition, such machines also require air-conditioning equipment which often uses more power than the computer itself. A microprocessor though, when connected to a VDU will consume energy at about the same rate as a domestic television. Micros can also be regarded as economic because they replace other energy extravagant systems of either a mechanical or an electromechanical nature. The ratio of materials used between a conventional system and that employing a micro can be greater than a thousand to one. For example, consider the simple circuit board that has replaced the mechanical cash register, or the banks of relays in a telephone exchange that will be superseded by a few cabinets of System X hardware. Not only have the resources required been dramatically reduced but also the amount of energy that the working product needs.

Because Information Technology only deals with data flow, it cannot in itself be a pollutant. It produces no material therefore there are no waste products and although some electricity is used, the amount is very small. Furthermore, microelectronics can provide the community with efficient pollution monitors, to help regulate the actions of other industrial processes and technologies. Although there will be instances where micros are incorporated into machines which are a source of pollution, they may help alleviate the situation. A micro in a motor car can improve engine efficiency, thereby reducing the need for lead additives to petrol. Microelectronics, whatever be its disadvantages, is a 'clean' technology, certainly in its use if not always in its manufacture.

Recycleability is another feature used to assess the appropriateness of particular tasks. It should be possible at the end of the useful life of a piece of equipment to salvage parts which can be redeployed, either directly or after some reprocessing. Unfortunately, if a microprocessor or memory chip ceases to function correctly it becomes worthless. Chips are not repairable, because they are too complicated and far too cheap. If the application becomes redundant, however, then the chips themselves can be reused; a circuit board is designed so that the individual elements can be easily fitted or removed. The memory (RAM) can be re-employed directly as it holds no information permanently. The processor can be then reprogrammed for a completely new task and even ROM (Read Only Memory) can be reused if it is of the EPROM (Erasable Programmable Read Only Memory) type. On a higher level, a microcomputer system containing VDU, keyboard, disc memory and printer can easily be split up and reallocated to new systems, if it cannot be redeployed as it is.

Microelectronics is environmentally sound and has a number of beneficial features appertaining to its application. The question of the social cost of usage is less clear cut. Chips neither give off dangerous chemicals nor radiation, they function on low voltages (although a mains supply is usually needed) and they have no moving parts. Therefore they would appear to be problem free. Printers and disc units which use mechanical elements could be a source of accidents, but the designers of these products have a good reputation in this respect. The only equipment which could cause some concern is the visual display unit (VDU), not a vital piece of equipment but one that is invariably part of any information processing equipment.

4.2.1 Hazards with VDUs

"The mental concentration and unfamiliar use of the eyes, which training personnel to operate VDUs entails, must be expected to cause eye strain in a large number of people." Ophthalmic optician for AOP (1979).

A study of 216 Air France VDU operators, undertaken by the French Institute of Health, found that over 10% of the operators suffered from some type of eye complaint, such as increased short-sightedness, colour vision trouble, redness of the eyes or stinging sensations. Nearly all the workers complained of eye strain. In Sweden, the National Board of Occupational Safety and Health conducted a survey of people engaged in 'full-time sedentary visual work'. They found that 75% felt discomfort in their eyes, 55% in their back and shoulders, 35% in their head and neck, 25% in their arms and wrists and 15% in their legs. It appears that although VDUs will not injure anyone seriously nor cause permanent blindness, they do represent a health hazard. It is in the interests of full-time operators, such as wordprocessor workers, that VDUs be designed correctly. In fact all users, including students at educational establishments, should understand the potential hazards of working with a VDU.

Early screens suffered from a number of design faults, they flickered, were noisy, 'wandered badly', and had poor colour clarity. They were used too close to the face and were usually stationed in an excessively bright room. A day's work on this type of equipment must have been akin to leaning forward slightly to watch an old television screen which has the sun shining on it and the volume turned up, for a period of seven and a half hours and at a focal distance of only twelve inches. This is clearly not conducive to good health. VDUs have improved considerably since the early designs but there is still a need for industrial standards and regular checks on the equipment.

The hazards faced by VDU operators are many. The most common complaint is general fatigue due to eye strain and uncomfortable posture. This can manifest itself in lack of job involvement, headaches, depression, loss of appetite, dizziness, indigestion, nervousness and insomnia, all of which would be mitigated if shift work were introduced in order to maximise financial return on expensive equipment. For serious migraine sufferers and TV-epileptics (these constitute only 5% of all epilectics) VDU flicker can be very distressing — they are advised not to use them. Because a VDU incorporates a cathode-ray tube there is a danger from radiation; X-ray, ultra-violet light and microwave. Of these, the presence of microwaves appear to be the most harmful since they can cause cataracts. From detailed considerations of VDU-based work by a number of organisations (usually union based), working conditions have been proposed which, if implemented, would go a long way towards counteracting the potential health hazards. The important topics are as follows:

Flicker and Glare

Many of the cheaper displays use a cathode-ray tube with short-persistence phosphorus as it is more durable. Unfortunately it also has a lower character refresh rate, which can cause noticeable flicker. A machine with a refresh rate of less than 50hz is not recommended as frequent servicing and the replacement of worn parts is essential. VDUs should be situated so that the screen does not reflect light, if possible it should have a glare index of less than 16. With personal computers, a common procedure is to attach a television for display purposes, this is not acceptable for equipment that is going to be used for many hours each day.

Temperature and Noise

VDUs generate heat from the tube and other assorted components. The early machines needed cooling fans to maintain an acceptable temperature internally. These were noisy and became increasingly irritating after long use. Modern sets, which rely more heavily on microelectronics, manage to keep the heat production down to such a level that a fan is not needed but they still give off some heat so adequate ventilation is necessary especially where units have been grouped together.

Positioning

The positioning of VDUs is particularly important. Because of the glare they should never be near a window and the lighting should be closely controlled.

In a normal office the lumination level is around 500 lux; for a room containing VDUs it should be much lower, almost 150 lux. It may help to have a separate light to shine on the desk top to ease the strain when looking at the script and arranged in such a way that it does not shine on the screen. Although the VDU should not be placed against a window it is essential that operators have an opportunity to rest their eyes by looking at objects at least twenty feet away. This could greatly reduce the incidence of eye strain.

Most VDUs are only available as complete fixed units which restricts the ability of the operator to find a comfortable working position. The best displays are those in which the keyboard and screen are detached and the angle of the screen can be altered. The right choice of chair type and desk height is also important as they can both greatly reduce posture and body fatigue. The ergonomics of the office has been the subject of considerable attention lately and is of particular significance in this area (Stewart 1977).

VET (VDU Eye Test)
Most unions recommend that operators have their eyes tested before starting work with VDUs and thereafter be tested once every two years, if under forty, and annually if over forty or if glasses are normally worn. A major factor affecting eye strain is the length of time an operator spends at the display. Many agreements have been reached in specific circumstances but there has been no overall policy in the commercial or the industrial sector. A typical local arrangement is that no operator should work more than two hours without a break, and that this break should be at least thirty minutes. In a working day no more than four to five hours should be spent before a screen.

Eye strain can affect anyone. However certain groups are recognised as being more susceptible, and recommendations have been made that people with astigmatism, and people who are long-sighted or wear bi-focal lenses should not work exclusively with VDUs. A number of unions, for example ASTMS, even advise that nobody over forty-five should regularly work with such equipment because eye trouble is more prevalent in older people.

Control
To return to the theme of user control, people who can choose the equipment themselves and decide the methods under which work will be done show fewer signs of the ill effects of working with VDUs (Birnbaum 1978). Some displays can be adjusted in height, position and screen angle and seating can be equally flexible. Decisions on when breaks should be taken, and what length they ought to be, should involve the operator. In more informal situations, such as at university, there must be some guidelines established to prevent the over-zealous user from damaging their eyes. With the equipment itself the colour, size of character, character matrix, keyboard design and software features are all factors best assessed by the user. Similarly, brightness and contrast, if easily adjustable, will alleviate user discomfort.

The VDU is here to stay, it will become as commonplace as the telephone and through videotex systems may have a regular place in many homes. Recent designs and work practices have shown that it can be used with minimal health risk, and one hopes that such standards will be carried across the industry. It should be remembered that for every typewriter replaced by a completely electronic device, large quantities of paper are saved.

4.3 USER DESIGN AND CONTROL

Since chips are manufactured by large multinational companies and incorporate sophisticated electronic circuitry, it may seem pointless to consider how an individual can design microprocessors; yet there are several ways in which users can exercise control over the microbased equipment with which they work. Although no individual could possibly hope to build a microprocessor, the micro should be regarded as raw material — a simple chip waiting to be directed wherever people see fit. It is not a technology nor tool until it is united with other equipment and programmed for the specified task. Users must become involved in this process if they wish to influence the end result in any way. In order to contribute to the design, a knowledge of the component parts is required, hence one must ask whether or not microelectronics can be sufficiently 'demystified' for the general public to understand its operation. The micro is a product of high technology and therefore, by definition, considerable skills are needed to fully interpret its workings and to plan its manufacture. However, there are conceptual models of computers and telecommunications which allow the user to become adequately familiar with the general structure of the 'new technology' as illustrated in Chapter 2. Computers are actually quite straightforward. They process data to obtain results by following well defined instructions. Knowledge of the semi-conductor properties of silicon is unnecessary at this level of understanding.

As was also indicated in Chapter 2, programming, which turns an inert processor into a working tool, is a devolved activity that all users can employ. To say that programming is an indigenous skill would be an exaggeration. Nevertheless it is becoming an increasingly common ability and will become more so, as educational establishments wake up to the need for such skills. By teaching children to program, one is not merely rectifying the shortage of qualified personnel nor are the children being brainwashed into accepting high technology; rather, community members are being shown how to control the technology around them. Programming as a skill does take time to acquire, but whilst it remains the monopoly of only a few, microelectronics will not evolve into a community technology.

Ideally, the situation would resemble the present relationship between a car and its owner; most people know, to a degree, how a car works although few would be able to construct one. Driving is a skill that, while by no means easy, most people can acquire if they wish and, once obtained, allows control over what the car does. To extend the analogy further, adaption, modification or repair of the vehicle are activities which can be undertaken by professional experts although, alternatively, most users can achieve much by a 'do-it-yourself' approach. While the user cannot even attempt to repair a microprocessor, he or she may find other adjustments, such as the addition of extra memory, well within their capabilities.

As microprocessor sales have enjoyed a steady increase, so has the publication of books and magazines dealing with computers in general and the small personal type in particular. From these, all the background technical and economic information a potential user might wish to know is readily available, including many introductory guides to programming. In addition, the government have provided some £55 million for its Microprocessor Application Project (MAPCON) to help any potential industrial user obtain feasibility studies and consultancy support for attempts to incorporate microtechnology when they have no 'in-house' expertise. As for the accessibility of the technology itself, this depends very much upon the application. Pocket calculators were at one time very expensive; now they are cheap enough to be available to all. Today, a few hundred pounds will buy you a microcomputer or a few pounds a week will rent one. Therefore they should be well within the budget of even the smallest organisation, if it has a need for such equipment.

As was mentioned earlier, the cost of participating in information systems, such as Prestel, can be prohibitively expensive for the individual. Every effort must be made, therefore, to persuade British Telecom to rethink its pricing policy and to encourage local institutions to make community links available with such services. Individuals who wish to use microelectronic equipment can be guided by books which advise upon various products. Programming texts are quite common too, hence the design and control of the technology to fulfil personal requirements is available. Unfortunately however, for most people, encounters with the 'new technology' frequently occur in the workplace where they have no say in the design or the control of the equipment. This need not be the case. In Norway, national agreements require firms to inform their workforce on all new developments and to encourage their participation in the initial design stages. Such negotiations are not just means to appease trade union power, for they genuinely provide greater flexibility and increased efficiency, which must be of benefit to the whole community. In order for Britain to emulate the Norwegian example, the traditional practice of management divulging as little as possible to its employees would have to be overcome.

In the previous section, the ergonomic design of computer equipment was described and the reasons for it being an important area of user concern in the past were discussed. This has largely been resolved by detailed studies but has led to the question of the appropriateness of the computer system design itself. If you are communicating with any kind of microbased equipment, such as an information system, control process or data processing unit, then you are participating in what has been called a man-machine or human-computer interface. This has been recognised as the weak link in many systems, the weakness stemming from poor documentation, lack of correct training for the personnel and the computer itself, which prints out meaningless messages and rarely appears to do what is required of it. Consider three user comments collected by the Applied Psychology Unit at Cambridge (Morton 1979):

"We come into contact with computer people, a great many of whom talk a very alien language, and you have constant difficulty in trying to sort out this kind of mid-Atlantic jargon."

"We were slung towards what in my opinion is a pretty inadequate manual and told to get on with it."

"We found we were getting messages back through the terminal saying there's not sufficient space on the machine. Now how in Hell's name are we supposed to know whether there's sufficient space on the machine?"

Everyone who has used a computer must, at one time or another, have been bewildered by some of the totally incomprehensible instructions emanating from the machine. The source of messages is not the hardware but the system software running in it. If you have not written these programs yourself or do not have access to them (which is usually the case), then as a user you have no way of interpreting the meaning of the computer's action. Attempts to remedy this position have centred upon the concept of *user-friendly* systems, where emphasis is placed on designing computer software to match the natural work pattern of the user (this is in contrast to the more normal experience whereby the users must fit in as best they can with the 'computer method'). With user-friendly systems messages are grammatically structured and, where possible, human commands, written in sentences, are analysed and obeyed if the correct meaning can be extracted. This compares favourably with traditional methods where a missing symbol of character would cause complete chaos. For example, a command which organises the output into pages given to one of the popular computers is the word:

PAPERTHROWS

but if, inadvertently, you type:

PAPERTHROW

the entire running program will terminate and any work done will be lost. A user-friendly system would know what was meant and proceed accordingly. One interpretation of the term 'friendly' has been to make the computer polite and endow it with apparently human characteristics. For instance, systems exist which present such messages as:

GOOD MORNING I HOPE YOU WILL HAVE A GOOD DAY

— which can be a little annoying especially if it is half past midnight and you have been working on the same program for the last fourteen hours!

Giving a computer a human face is not the same as making it user-friendly; in many instances it is quite the reverse, because the limitations of the system, which should be apparent to the user, can be hidden behind a series of inane platitudes. With educational systems, every effort is put into making the computers appear human in the belief that school pupils will react better to such machines. Whether this will be detrimental to the understanding of the working, function and role of the technology has not yet been analysed. Computer messages must, naturally, be phrased in the native language and give precise indications as to what is occurring, offering a choice of actions to the user. The essential feature of a friendly system is that it should dissipate the traditional concept of the computer as a 'black box', the user in a 'white collar' and a limited set of rigid, explicit messages passing between them. Instead of this, the user and the machine become part of the same system, with the interaction being two-way. The computer software is written so that it can both interpret user statements and anticipate problems, and, perhaps more importantly, it presents a 'human window' to the user who can see exactly what is happening and can ask an unlimited amount of questions to enhance his or her understanding of the computer's functioning.

Although an ideal situation might be one in which users compose their own programs all the time, this is obviously impractical and inefficient. It is senseless for someone to spend weeks perfecting, say, a stock control package if this effort is a duplication of previous similar programs already designed by others for similar tasks. Alterntively, the purchasing of an 'off-the-shelf' program which does not perform exactly as you would wish or, even worse, fails to work properly for the kind of problem posed is far from satisfactory. A compromise between these two positions may come from buying standard software and then adapting it to one's particular needs.[†] To do this, the program must be written in a high level language with which you are familiar. For most microcomputers there are a large number of programs, written in the common language BASIC, which can perform all manner of tasks. If one can program in BASIC then one can easily understand and alter these programs according to one's own specifications.

However, many firms who sell software, especially of the business application variety, prefer to keep their programs 'hidden' by releasing only the machine-code version which although it runs correctly, is neither readable nor adaptable. The reasons for adopting this market approach are to protect their products from being copied and resold, and to encourage the customer to become dependent upon the company's software. Commercial software packages exist which are so rigid in their specifications and design that each time the rate of VAT (Value

---

[†] Another technique is discussed in the next section.

Added Tax) changes, a new version of the program has to be bought from the supplier. So often the user has come to depend on their computer facility and having no control over the software, she or he must pay whatever price the retailer demands. This type of software is inappropriate for virtually all applications.

Dependence upon the hardware can also be of concern. Although micro-computers are available in all kinds of shapes, sizes and costs, the range of choice for large computers, telecommunication links, satellites and information systems is very much narrower. The use of a technology should not entail the introduction of external cultural influences. In the 1978 NORA report, the French government were warned that IBM was such a powerful company that it could dictate the type of equipment and services to be used in the western world. Attempts to limit IBM's power by the US government have, in the past, failed. Does an increased dependence upon foreign hardware and telecommunications systems constitute an undue influence on our culture?

As knowledge about microtechnology permeates through society, with programming and system design becoming commonplace tasks, the opportunities for individuals to design applications, or at least have control over the systems they use, will increase. Whether the realisation of these opportunities will prove damaging to employment prospects depends largely on the extent to which 'new technology agreements' are negotiated on the shop floor and the degree of pressure that can be placed on designers to create truly participatory computer systems. A further look at systems analysis will be given in the next chapter.

4.4 FLEXIBILITY, CREATIVITY AND VISION

From the many applications considered so far, it must be clear that micro-electronic devices can be useful in all manner of industrial processes and products, and all aspects of information handling. This may show that the concept of the micro is flexible but is it true to say that any particular micro is multi-purpose? After all, the wheel has many uses but the versions found on the bicycle and tractor are not interchangeable. As described earlier, many chips are re-usable because they perform standardised functions; for example, a memory chip could operate equally well in a variety of microcomputers as could a chip which automatically computes a Fourier analysis. The real flexibility of the microprocessor lies in its ability to be programmed for different tasks. The same physical device is thus capable of a multitude of roles, each dependent upon the instructions issued.

It has already been mentioned that microprocessor based equipment comes in two basic types, *programmable* and *embedded*. The kind of system to which each are applied will now be discussed. Embedded systems are suited to quite a few tasks but their disadvantage lies in the fact that the user has little control over the computing part of the equipment, which in turn reduces his or her influence over the way it operates. The micro-based system that mixes the correct amount of air and petrol in the engine of a motor car can save considerable fuel, and its stored program is so straightforward that no significant benefit could be gained from allowing the user of the car to reprogram it. Other embedded systems, such as an automatic washing machine, can have a wide range of inputs which would enhance the machine's diversity. New washing techniques however, such as cold temperature powders, cannot usually be accomodated, for even though the washer could be adapted to these new methods, it would first need to be reprogrammed. In a complicated scheme such as a large building heating system, an embedded processor would not be sufficiently flexible to change the operational algorithms or set-points and would therefore not be appropriate.

One argument against this type of flexibility is that the user would have to know how to program in order to realise this amount of control over the equipment. This is partly because even if schools become aware of the need to teach programming, it will be a long time before a significant proportion of the population could acquire this skill. Between the two extremes of programmable and embedded systems rest a number of alternative strategies, one of which is called *program-generation*. Here, instructions are not given to the processor in the form of a complete program, but rather as data to an existing program. Program-generation differs from standard data input in that the existing program actually propagates a new one which incorporates the user's specifications; this can then be run as an ordinary program.

Data are presented to the generator in the form of dialogue, in which all the parameters of the required system are described and the structure for the output or results chosen. For example, consider the production of a program which would simulate the heat flow from an ordinary house, using a variety of possible heating systems. For any particular house, a straightforward program could be written to assess such factors as room temperature; and produce some predictions as to heat loss, cost or overall efficiency. Because it has been designed for one specific house, this program cannot be used for other buildings with different dimensions or numbers of rooms. If a program which could be run for all houses were created, it would be inefficient in a number of ways and contain substantial amounts of redundant code. With a generating technique, a 'parent' program would ask for all relevant information on a new house and then produce a new program, custom built to undertake the analysis required. The generated program would usually be much smaller than the parent and would fit onto a microcomputer, even if the parent would not.

It is not easy to devise generator programs as they must obviously be more sophisticated then their ensuing offspring; in particular the design of the dialogue by which the non-specialist can describe her or his requirements can be quite a problem. Nevertheless, if enough thought and planning are put into its production, a versatile program which can be used widely, should result. Individual programs, because of their specific nature, may never be used sufficiently to reduce their commercial price. General purpose software packages may also only sell in small numbers because they fail to meet particular needs. A stock control generator, for example, could produce specific programs to meet such needs, and become very popular. In doing so it would make a genuine contribution towards cheaper software.

In order that the user be as familiar as possible with the system, both the original and the ensuing programs of the generator scheme in particular must be written in a language the user can understand. The previous section (4.3) described how, even for an experienced programmer, alterations to a standard package can be less time consuming than writing one from scratch. Program generation is a quick way of getting close to the required software:

> "Cincom, the leading independent data base vendor, will have a program generator on the market early in the new year (1981) which could replace about eighty per cent of COBOL programs." – Computing.

Embedded systems, because they do not have to provide facilities to allow reprogramming, will invariably be cheaper than fully programmable equipment and in many cases this is to the consumer's benefit. In future, standardisation of micro based equipment, especially in the area of common interfaces, may make quite ordinary applications reprogrammable by the user or a local engineer. The flexibility of the convivial computer depends upon the development of multipurpose hardware and software.

With embedded systems the degree to which the user can express creativity and vision is also restricted and must depend upon the equipment, and not the micro situated inside it. The use of microelectronics can extend the scope of such equipment but this is just as likely to limit creativity. Expression and vision are possible in systems which are programmable and where the user is involved with the application design. A computer program is a problem description, in a language which contains a large number of conceptual tools not available in any national tongue. To speak and understand a foreign language is, in itself, creative and this is similarly the case with computer languages. Even pure problem solving, such as completing a crossword, is considered by many to be inspirational. Nearly everyone who has learnt to program finds it an enjoyable, rewarding and addictive pursuit.

Technology can be regarded in the light of an evolutionary rather than a revolutionary process. Man's adjustment to the environment has resulted in the invention of tools designed to compensate for our physical limitations. Illustrations of this can be found throughout history but more recent ones include the harnessing of external energies to improve our muscular abilities; for example, the steam engine brought about the speedy transportation of travellers and merchandise. Likewise, electricity, in the form of television, radio and telephone, has extended our senses. So far our self-improvement plans have been concentrated around physical constraints. Microelectronic technology, however, is an attempt to perfect our mental capabilities. Information technology offers greater data storage than the brain can accomodate and a more efficient retrieval system. Computers can analyse problems too difficult for our comprehension and undertake tasks beyond our concentration. The micro is not, however, a substitute for the brain anymore than a pneumatic drill is for our muscles or a car for our legs; it should expand our abilities not restrict or replace them.

Many writers have used the idea of advanced technologies to experiment with different social orders and community structures. Any vision of the future must take microelectronics into account, whilst at the same time defining a framework for the microbased technologies so that it will fit into this vision. This section will be concluded by relating two hypothetical descriptions of the possible relationship between society and advanced technology.

Microprocessors for a Parallel Culture

"There is evidence that the conventional type of industrial society which provides the model for world development does not comply with the logic of a finite world with a fragile ecology. . .

The methodology for designing alternative cultures is known as structural sociotechnics, the study of the inter-relationship between social organisations and technological artefacts.

So far this process has been largely technology dominated with social patterns being adapted to technological innovation. The opposite approach is to define a desired type of social system and to design technological artefacts to support it.

The role of the microprocessor can be very important in structural sociotechnics since it can be used for a wide variety of purposes at the behest of the social designer." (MIPAC – unpublished paper 1980)

This organisation MIPAC, based in Edinburgh, is concerned with the society of the future, but unlike many other 'alternative' groups it is not anti-technology; on the contrary it is prepared to put informatics at the centre of the culture. Without analysing in too greater detail the structure of alternative societies, it is interesting to note one of the main roles anticipated for the micro. A tenet of any decentralised community is the need to have free and easy communications throughout the society. MIPAC has been considering how information technology can help keep people up to date and give every individual in society the facility and opportunity to participate in the decisions which will affect him or her.

By way of an example, MIPAC are hoping to organise themselves on a microcomputer network so that everyone interested in, or working on, components of 'parallel cultures' can easily compare findings and so eliminate any duplication, thus helping the work to progress more quickly. The obvious medium for this network is Prestel but costs might prohibit this. As much work on alternative technologies is concerned with building and machinery design where the ability to pass diagrams and documents through the telecommunication network would be crucial and, as the amount of data grows, flexible indexing and 'search' software will become increasingly important. MIPAC is mainly concerned with the philosophical aspects of future social structures (the next scheme is a more pragmatic one). Its ideas are, however, based upon the existence of the kind of technology that will sustain these structures.

Protopia : a Community for the Future

Many sociologists and technologists interested in the inherent problems of modern communities have postulated on what would constitute an appropriate plan for the 'village of tomorrow'. One team has gone beyond the general idea to produce a detailed blueprint and, in 1980, exhibit a model of their findings. Andrew Page of this group explained the background thus:

> "It aims at a creative synthesis of the telematic revolution now upon us and the 'green' or ecological movement. For a year now I have been 'grounding' the highly theoretical aspects of Protopia. Supported by a bursary from the Dartington Hall Trust, I have been preparing an exhibition, Tomorrows Village, whose centrepiece is a 1:250 scale model of a 'Community for the Future'." (Page 1980)

Protopia is not meant to be a real-life plan for a future village but rather a 'thinkpiece' to focus discussion and debate. It is designed for a community of approximately 2,000 that, to a large extent, would be self-sufficient and locally governed. High and low technologies are mixed as is the work that members of the community are expected to undertake. The main elements of the model are:

1. High density housing: well insulated and with solar-powered water heating.
2. Central market place.
3. Cafe and pub combined.
4. Multi-purpose village hall.
5. Library.
6. Creche and nursery school.
7. Outlook tower — 'symbol of spiritual aspiration.'
8. Health spa.
9. Inn and hotel for visitors.
10. Workshops.
11. Aquaculture centre.
12. Windmills.
13. Allotments.
14. Cottage office.
15. Learning centre.

The last two items are particularly relevant to the theme of this book, so it is worth describing them in more detail.

Cottage Office

> "A 'resource centre' offering computer facilities, public telephone, message centre and answering service, and television with Teletext and Viewdata and other link-ups. . ." (Page 1980)

The whole activity of the computer village is linked together by a network of personal computers. People wanting work can interrogate a data base on which people offering work have placed jobs, (which in this context imply single tasks not full-time jobs). The size of the job, rate of remuneration, skills required etc. are all stored on the computer. When an individual has selected a task, she or he communicates their agreement to the 'employer' who will, when the job is complete, remove it from the data base and arrange for the proper amount of money transferred between the two bank accounts concerned. Banking is an automated function of the cottage office. Other functions that are attributed to the information system are the analysis of local market fluctuations, the co-ordination of major projects, a universal referenda program (DEMOS) for instant expression of majority views, and a monitor of energy usage.

With such an organised information system there are obvious difficulties in effectively defining its role. The dividing line between a system which promotes efficiently co-ordinated work and one that controls and dictates activity is indeed a thin one. It is not clear what safeguards are envisaged in Protopia.

Learning Centre

"Learning and skills sharing (secondary, university level and adult education) utilising television, Open University and Open School, and computers within personal tutorial programmes. . . " (Page 1980)

Education in Protopia is considered a life-long activity. Many of the skills learnt in the village workshop will be of the practical variety, but there will also be considerable emphasis placed on more formal learning, and this will mainly be centred on computerised educational schemes emanating from outside the village. More general education information will be available via the village viewdata system which is accessible to all residents. Where appropriate, library material will be stored electronically to save space and paper. The learning centre and cottage office are the two elements of the village which are distinctly high technology. By comparison, much of the industry and work will be of the intermediate or low variety so as to provide sufficient employment. Work is shared, the unpleasant jobs offer the highest pay and must, in time, be undertaken by all, (no indication is given of how the community would deal with someone who didn't). The emphasis of the village is on personal development, through an integrative structure and involvement, and an appreciation of nature. To organise such a community, the designers of Protopia have decided that a microelectronic based information system is appropriate.

Protopia is a vision of the future and, moreover, it is made possible by the existence of microelectronics. The micro can lead to flexible aids, can be made with no social cost, and used safely if health standards are understood and adhered to: this is the basis of a convivial or appropriate tool. There remains one question, however, what can you actually do with it?

5

Socially Useful Applications

The most fundamental characteristic which a technology must have if it is to be termed 'appropriate' is the ability to fulfil a socially useful task. Regardless of whether they prove socially beneficial, all technologies are concerned with the transformation of technique and knowledge. Microelectronics is no exception to this but, as has been described, the micro is the raw material for many technologies, some of which are obviously inappropriate whilst others are of immense use. This chapter will give some practical illustrations of microtechnology in action. These particular applications have been chosen to indicate the wide variety of tasks that small, efficient computers can undertake. This list however is by no means exhaustive.

Like the large computer, the micro is an information processor, it takes in data and produces results by following simple instructions. However the significance of the input, and the form and consequence of the output can be very different. The previous chapter described how the deployment of microtechnology can have many basic ecological benefits, and enhance individuality, flexibility and creativity. It is now useful to discuss such factors within the framework of actual applications. The main areas in which computers have so far shown themselves to be of use are:

1. Analysis — numerical.
2. Analysis — systems organisation.
3. Public information systems.
4. Personal data processing.
5. Monitoring and control.
6. Entertainment.

I shall endeavour to present a detailed example of these areas, to illustrate how to apply advanced technology, and indicate the benefits that could accrue from a positive attitude toward the micro.

5.1 NUMERICAL ANALYSIS

The initial tasks of ENIAC, the world's first fully electronic computer, were concerned with the solution of difficult mathematical problems and to this day a major use of computing technology is still numerical analysis. Atom bomb design and ballistic trajectories were the first two applications of this new technology. Since then most scientific and engineering work has come to depend upon the assistance of large computers in the design and testing of ideas and equipment. Whilst computing costs have decreased, the theory of numerical analysis has evolved and the sophistication of software has improved. Other fields of study have, however, become very expensive either because of the time needed to perform the necessary calculations by hand, or because of the cost of developing equipment. The result of this is that an increasing amount of effort and time is spent analysing computer models rather than experimental ones.

For example, take one area of engineering application, the design of heat storage systems. In many industrial processes, thermal energy can be recovered from waste gas and re-cycled within the industry to improve its overall efficiency by reducing fuel requirements. As well as being of immediate benefit to that industry, the savings to the whole community in terms of energy consumption can be considerable if waste heat recovery becomes widely used. Many environmentalists even argue that by attacking this area alone, sufficient savings could be made to delay the need for a nuclear power programme, for at least a hundred years. One method of heat recovery is to pass the hot waste gas, from some industrial process, through a series of pipes, adjacent to which are a further set of pipes in which a cool fluid flows. Heat passes from the hot gas to the cooler material, which can then be used for either space heating or in other processes. A disadvantage of this method is that the heat has to be used at the same time as it is produced. If there is not a constant requirement for this heat, it would be better to pass the hot gas through some heat retaining substance and store it for future use. Heat could then be recovered by passing a cold gas, or in some instances a liquid, back through this material to extract the stored heat. This system, illustrated in Fig. 5.1, is called a regenerator and there can be domestic as well as industrial benefits from the application of regenerators:

> "At present some 50% of domestic water heating energy is lost with the waste water; most of this could be reclaimed, giving a saving of about 30 million MWh of useful energy, about 2% of UK present primary energy." (NCAT 1978)

Regenerators can also be used to store and release solar energy. Solar power arrives during the day but is usually needed more in the evenings and night; consequently the heat needs to be retained. On a longer time scale, thermal stores which attempt to hold enough 'summer heat' to be of value in the winter, are also exhibiting regenerative behaviour, although in this example it is customary for water to be used to hold the heat, whereas most industrial techniques employ a ceramic material as a heat retainer.

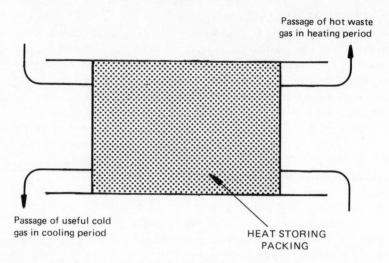

Passage of hot waste
gas in heating period

Passage of useful cold
gas in cooling period

HEAT STORING
PACKING

Fig. 5.1 – Diagrammatic representation of a regenerator.

It should be clear from this that the regenerator is an important device and that a full understanding of its operation and design would be of great benefit in energy conservation. One advantage of studying the behaviour of a system such as a regenerator is that results obtained can be applied to a wide variety of applications. An industrial regenerator has entirely different operating conditions to that of a domestic thermal store and yet, from a computer model's point of view, the difference is one of parameter values. A single computer program could produce accurate information to assist in designing regenerators of whatever magnitude.

To develop a computer model for any physical system, a mathematical description of the actual processes which are taking place must first be produced. For the regenerator, this was first achieved in the 1920s when small pieces of heat storing material were analysed for their ability to absorb and emit heat. The whole regenerator was then considered to be the sum action of all the minute pieces which constitute it. After approximating some activities and making assumptions about others, a set of mathematical equations were derived which described the regenerator's activities. There are two types of behaviour that a regenerator can exhibit. Given constant operating conditions it will eventually operate consistently; alternatively if the operating conditions are continually changing (as they would in a domestic environment) then the regenerator performance will vary also. Before the availability of computers it was just possible, after many hours of work, to obtain results on steady state conditions but not on transient behaviour. By 1964, algorithms and computer programs were available for anyone who had access to a large computer. If one required a regenerator to deal with a certain amount of waste heat, guarantee 95% heat absorbtion, and not become saturated after three weeks of very hot weather, the computer simulation would give quick and accurate design measurements. The alternative was either to trust inaccurate calculations or to build the biggest regenerator possible to be on the safe side.

The numerical algorithm used to predict behaviour, although based upon sophisticated techniques, is quite simple and needs a computer program of less than fifty statements. One run of the program would, in less than a second, provide a theoretical prediction of thermal efficiency for whatever parameters were input. By comparison, in 1930 a famous German engineer undertook with his wife, friends and family a similar calculation — it took them more than six weeks. What is more, one need no longer have a large mainframe computer at one's disposal because the program will now fit onto a programmable calculator.

Although steady state calculations furnish the designer with a very good idea of the required size and material characteristics needed to construct a regenerator, in reality the operating conditions under which it must work are rarely constant. Recent work has shown that the overall efficiency of this type of storage system is very much influenced by variations in the environment in which it works. For example, if a heat store is to be used to transmit summer heat to winter, it must be able to deal with a diverse selection of weather prospects. No store, in Britain, would be expected to give total winter heating after even a glorious summer, but one might want a system that could guarantee 50% of winter heat in 85% of years. Again, in minutes, a computer program could simulate fifty years of weather conditions to test the effectiveness of a proposed thermal unit.

In addition to helping the designer, once a system is working a computer simulation can be employed to test various operating proposals in order to indicate whether or not there are any unforeseen difficulties. In the iron making process, waste heat from the blast furnace has, for many years, been used to pre-heat the actual blast. A change in operating conditions here can and has caused considerable damage to the plant, due to the gas temperatures becoming uncontrollable. Computer analysis can predict the likely outcome in such circumstances and perhaps save millions of pounds worth of equipment as well as helping the furnace run with greater efficiency. In heating up the blast to the required temperature of approximately 1500 C, considerable quantities of oil and gas are consumed; the more effective the waste heat recovery then the greater the saving in finite resources.

All the analysis required to describe regenerator behaviour can be accomplished on a microcomputer; the mathematics can at times be difficult because the problem is intrinsically awkward and complicated. Numerical analysis is concerned with turning mathematical relationships into computer simulated solutions. Many of the techniques available are not easy to prove but they can be used, in terms of software packages, in general design work. Similarly, statistical programs can undertake quite complex data analysis. In both these fields where there is an inherent danger in using techniques which one does not fully understand; well written software should help by indicating the correct and incorrect application areas. If a technology is complex then there is no alternative but to apply complex tools and the microcomputer can be one of these aids. Numerical analysis was, for many years, the major area of computer use, although this has now been superseded by data processing applications. Another sphere of computer influence is that of the monitoring and control of equipment, which invariably requires some form of analysis to transform input data into output commands. Products can be found in both these applications which are socially motivated, like the regenerator, although others can be found which are not.

5.2 SYSTEMS ANALYSIS

Numerical work may in the past have been the forte of the computer but, shortly after such machines became available, the data processing function came to the fore, and this remains the position today. Systems analysis is concerned with the structure and organisation of any system, be it commercial, business, industrial, institutional, domestic or political. As the structure of an organisation is formed by and reflected in the flow of internal information, it is not surprising that computing technology is closely concerned with the application of this analysis. In British universities, systems analysis is a course found extensively in the computer science department not, for example, in sociology or economics although it is concerned with the interaction of individuals, and the economic efficiency of business.

With cheap microelectronic equipment, there is now a wide choice as to how the information flow should be organised within a company structure. It is no longer necessary to exclusively use large, centrally based data processing divisions built upon a single mainframe computer. Information can be situated or routed to where it is needed. This can greatly affect how the large institutions are organised and hence this area of micro application is potentially the most significant of all.

5.2.1 Small Business Systems

Although systems analysis is primarily concerned with overall structural organisation, to give an indication of the type of task the microcomputer can perform in the commercial sector one needs to examine some small stand-alone office aids.

Automated Filing Cabinet

It is customary for any service industry to keep a record of clients so that it can best serve their needs whilst, at the same time, maximising its own business. Typically a filing cabinet is used, and records are kept giving the customer's name, address, age, sex and then a list of characteristics which describe and categorise the customer in terms of items important to the organisation. For instance, an educational establishment would have previous qualifications, present courses etc; a community centre might include members interests, skills and 'free time' as well as the subscription renewal date. The sales representative would split customers between the products they buy and the area in which they reside, and an insurance broker would consider his or her clients in terms of profession, type of policy obtained and income bracket.

What all of these have in common is that once the filing system exceeds a certain size, it becomes unworkable. When there are only a few hundred records then it is possible to look through them quite quickly and identify the person with the sought after characteristics. When the client population grows into thousands, however, the doors of the cabinet tend to stay firmly closed or, at best, are only opened to insert new names. A microcomputer can alleviate this situation, by one of two methods.

The simplest way is to keep the filing cabinet and use the microcomputer solely as an indexer and cross-referencer. New clients have a physical record made out as before but, in addition, brief details are entered onto the computer to be stored on floppy discs. When it becomes necessary to find, for example, all left handed snooker players who are free on Friday evenings, a simple command at the VDU will list on the line printer all possible members. To obtain further information about each person on the list, such as their address, the filing cabinet is used, as it can provide more detailed data. The advantage of this method is that full records are still kept on a physical medium, whilst the ordinarily time-consuming searches through records can be performed in seconds by a computer.

Many analysts, when faced with the problem of an unusable filing system, will advise that the whole manual system be replaced. All data, including addresses and ancillary notes, are now stored on the computer, the advantages being that it is compact, saves time previously spent writing out and searching through records and, with a good printer, envelopes and letters can be automatically generated. The computer here is working as a wordprocessor as well as a data processor. Against these advantages, one must bear in mind that the increased data storage might necessitate a larger, more expensive computer system; floppy discs may no longer be adequate and a hard disc unit may be required.

The software for a simple record keeping system can be bought at a reasonably low cost and adapted to the user's needs with few problems. The hardware for a small computer was described in Chapter 2 and would be quite adequate for many applications of the indexing and cross-referencing type. One feature that the microcomputer must possess for this kind of application is *random access files*. This means records can be placed on the discs in a way that will allow individual entries to be extracted with ease. For example, if the ninety-seventh record was required it could be asked for directly: without random access the first ninety-six records would have to be read and discarded before the ninety-seventh became available.

It may not appear that automating an office filing system is a socially beneficial aspect of the micro, yet the efficient running of any organisation must be advantageous. Many institutions would benefit greatly from having closer liaison with their members, clients or customers. Groups interested in technology would undoubtedly find it useful to keep a record of people interested in their work and to whom information should be sent. A small list is easy but an extensive one, in which the people concerned have a variety of interests, is much more difficult to organise by hand. A central body that monitored publications and recorded useful titles under headings such as: third world, energy/wind, heat recovery etc. would be invaluable. As was mentioned earlier, this type of service has already been established, categorising individual interests within specific academic areas, and there is no reason why it should not expand. In local libraries, a computer system would be a highly flexible alternative to the present card files or microfiche, especially as the library records are becoming increasingly computerised. Useful 'searching' software would lead to greater access to information and this must be socially beneficial.

For large amounts of data the capacity of the microcomputer is exceeded and a minicomputer becomes necessary. Although much more expensive, applications can and do warrant such outlay. It depends on the price placed on being 'informed' or working efficiently. A filing cabinet may be full of data but it is valueless unless it is organised and used.

Production Schedulers

There are two tales often told in commercial computer circles which clearly illustrate the benefits and pitfalls which can ensue from the use of computer equipment. One is of the fellow so impressed by a computer salesman that he decides to convert all his accounts to one automated scheme. The salesman (representing the hardware firm selling the equipment) assures the client that the programs would be easy to write, and that a local software-house will no doubt undertake the task for him. The manager/owner of our small firm buys the machine and software, retires his ageing accounting staff and waits to see his profits grow. In nine months he is bankrupt. The computing system never worked properly and the manufacturer and the software-house blamed each other for the faults. He could not attract his staff back and because he had no idea of how to program and very little knowledge of accounts. He could not see where the problems were, he lost track of money that was owed to him and could not meet his debts — one of which was for the computer.

The second tale concerns a manufacturer who is concerned with the cash flow and production organisation of the firm. She buys a small microcomputer system with software, from the same source, learns to at least understand programming, and runs the automated scheme next to the manual one for a long trial period. Because well laid out bills go out on time and production is more efficient the computer system pays for itself in two months. The firm is organised more effectively, retains its staff, produces a more flexible product range and can give a more informed customer service.

The moral of these tales, which crop up in various guises, is to fit the computer system to the task, understand its role and do not abandon the existing system until one is completely happy with the automated version. There are a number of business tasks amenable to computer centred organisation, such as the sales ledger and the pay office. The next application is of a production scheduler as this can have ramifications upon all of a company's work force. The model is based upon a working system (Kirkham 1980).

A small manufacturer employs twenty people to make, let us say, thirty different types of mountings for heat pumps. Orders are recieved from all parts of the country and are delivered by the firm's own transport. It usually takes two days to make a mounting and fifteen are completed each day. The normal delivery date is three to four weeks after the order has been placed. As it is more efficient to make mountings of the same type on any particular day, there is the difficulty of planning production in order to maximise output. With the manual system, the head of the firm spent considerable time of each week planning the following week's production. He was faced with the five difficulties:

1. For efficient transport use, the vans should be full when leaving the factory and should deliver in only one geographical area; this was not easy to organise.
2. Production sheets had to be transcribed many times and this was cumbersome on the shop floor.
3. Schedules were inflexible and it was not easy to rearrange them to meet special orders.
4. Customer enquiries were difficult to deal with as the progress of any one item was never easily to hand.
5. It took two full days to work out the schedule for a week.

As the company expanded it became clear that the manual system would not suffice. A microcomputer was purchased with a VDU, a printer and a dual mini-floppy disc unit; software was then developed which matched the clerical procedures previously employed. After some initial difficulties, scheduling became entirely automated, orders were manually fed into the computer which then produced a weekly production scheme. From the firms point of view, the following effects were apparent:

1. Orders were completed is less time.
2. The vans were dispatched with greater loads and to a more confined geographical area.
3. The workforce had access to the VDU on which to report the progress of work and to view the production schedule.

4. It became possible to rearrange production at a minutes notice, if the situation arose.
5. The progress of a customer's order was easily obtained, all that was needed was for the order number to be entered on the VDU.
6. The whole process of producing the weekly schedule now took very little time.

In addition, at any time the microcomputer could produce reports on any part of the manufacturing process, such as all orders of type X waiting to be delivered. With this type of information to hand, the manager could supervise the manufacture and spend more time planning the overall company strategy rather than the day to day tactics.

This type of equipment is both a production scheduler and a management information system, but there is no reason why the shop floor VDU (if different from that of the managers) should not have all company information on it. In this way the workforce could keep track of production and participate in the firm's activities. For our heat pump manufacturer, a 20% increase in deliveries was witnessed in the first month of full computer operation.

Any organisation concerned with planning activities faces difficulties in efficiently dividing the tasks to be done between people who can do them, in the time available. This is especially true if the organisation is such that no one person is responsible for scheduling the work activities of everybody else. A small computer system can act as a focal point in such concerns and through the flexibility of its software, production can be planned and replanned to match changing situations. If the activities themselves are socially beneficial then their efficient organisation must also be.

5.2.2 Holistic View
It should be apparent, particularly from the last example, that the acquisition of a microcomputer can have an effect upon the whole structure of a company. One micro can alter the entire accounting, production and management functions and this is why systems analysis is unavoidably linked to the application of microtechnology. Telecommunications links and large computerised data bases are obviously of even greater significance to organisational structure.

In many ways the term 'systems analysis' is a contradictory one, for *analysis* implies the method of reduction and splitting up of a problem into smaller parts which can each then be dealt with individually. The *system* approach is, however, one of completeness. It suggests a holistic[†] view by looking at the entire structure at one go and tackling the problem where it stands. The reductionist procedure is easier, furnishing the analsyst as it does with a number of powerful tools which have proved very successful in the studies of physics, chemistry and engineering. One area where it has failed is in the social sciences,

[†]From *holism* – a tendency to form wholes that are more than the sum of their parts.

for with these systems the organisation is not just the sum of its parts. The inter-relationships between system elements are more important than the elements themselves and can only be studied by looking at the whole complex. Systems analysis is concerned with the information flow within an entire structure and therefore has generally adopted a holistic modus operandi.

Systems analysis, based upon a holistic approach is usually taken to mean the consideration of the following three steps:

1. Identify the larger system (suprasystem) of which the system in question is a part.
2. Explain the behaviour of the suprasystem.
3. Explain the role and functions of the system in question within the suprasystem.

An analyst, when asked to look at the workings of one part of an organisation, will first consider the whole concern and, if necessary, search for a larger suprasystem of which the organisation is a part. The process is one of progressively defining larger containing systems until the stage where the new system is completely beyond one's control. Once the environment is thus defined the concerned structure can be examined through its interaction with the whole. In order to achieve this, detailed observation, especially of the information flow, is required. Many tools and methodologies are available to the systems analyst and the primary objective is to identify the purpose of the system. Invariably, the analyst is called in by management and, as Ackoff (1978) relates:

> "The management of an organisation involves taking into account (1) the organis-ation's purposes – the *self-control* problem; (2) the purpose of its parts – the *humanization* problem; and (3) the purpose of the containing system(s) – the *environmentalization* problem. Until recently, managers, and those who serve them, have focussed almost exclusively upon the first of these problems." (his italics)

Although the analyst's function is to devise an organisation or plan that will best reflect the purposes of the system, the description of efficient information flow does not necessarily contain a recommendation of the appropriate computer equipment to buy. A microcomputer-based production scheduler, such as the one featured earlier, may have been the correct solution for the particular firm, but often the analyst will recommend no change. Many business succeed because certain members of staff lunch together or car-share on the way to work; for them formalised information control would not improve anything. Yet it is true to say that the goal of many systems workers is to design the perfect computer centred MIS – Management Information System. Informatics should be able to offer the manager all the data she or he needs to do the job, which is to control and orchestrate. Unfortunately, the record of MIS has so far been rather poor.

Where, you may ask, is the beneficial micro in all this? For the answer one must look at a typical large company or corporation which tends to have only a handful of real decision makers, because such people need to be 'informed'. The type of structure that has evolved to meet this need is found in most institutions; whereby layers of management filter specialised information to the point at which it can be co-ordinated to assist the executive in a decision making capacity. With information systems based on distributed telecommunications and micro driven displays, alternative structures can be designed in such a way as to increase the number of people who can participate in the policy and decision-making process. Additionally, the last two problems highlighted by Ackoff, namely those of *humanisation* and *environmentalisation*, can be included in the system dynamics. A MIS could be extended to involve the total organisation which could then identify the consequences of the differing motivations and purposes of the subsystem, system and suprasystem; that is to say, the institution itself, those who work within it and the environment in which it exists.

An alternative to hierarchical control, which has had an equally long history, is the co-operative model. Here the centralised structure is dismantled and all the participants have an equal say in and, where applicable, remuneration from the venture. The co-operative method undoubtedly works on a small scale but has been impossible to apply to the diverse institutions with hundreds or even thousands of members. Decision making in a co-operative is usually based on weekly meetings, the purpose of which is to keep everyone informed of all activities and to democratically plan the following week's work. Large meetings would have great difficulty in fulfilling this function.

Decentralisation, which is what the co-operative model entails for all but the small organisations, requires systems which can 'inform' large numbers of people and so enable them to express their views. To install an information system which can recieve data from various sources, allow this data to be challenged or changed and to link together physically separate groups, requires telecommunication links, computer hardware and well designed software. The use of microtechnology is insufficient to supervise a move towards decentralisation but it is a prerequisite. In Scandinavia, where participation and industrial democracy are becoming the norm and worker consultations are even required by law, the computer has acquired a new role, that of a disseminator rather than a concentrator.

5.3 PUBLIC INFORMATION SYSTEMS AND INDIVIDUAL COMPUTER USAGE

Systems analysis is primarily concerned with the structural organisation of well defined institutions, such as companies or government departments. Outside this area, lie the larger systems of the community and the smaller units such as the individual or the nuclear family. A systems analysis approach could be attempted on the whole society, an example of which will be related below, but in general such a task would be impossible because of the size of the system under examination. One is therefore left with the problem of having to assess each technology or information system in its own right, and trying to predict the likely impact of its application.

The computerisation of familiar aspects of our day to day lives brings with it the possibilty of substantial social change and community reorganisation, which could even challenge the structure of our market economy and the organisation of our democratic controls. For example, as Bodington pointed out, it is now

> "technically possible for individuals and groups of consumers to communicate their requirements through computerised information exchanges; to which producers would communicate their availabilities and from which they would receive suitable processed information about demands. This would not be barter, but a form of reaching understanding, a new model of social relations to replace the market." (Bodington 1974)

It is doubtful whether Prestel could precipitate such a dramatic change in our social order, but the French are of the opinion that Informatics will cause major alterations to the way the nation functions. Within the scope of such changes there must be room for the decentralised, appropriate application of information systems to counteract the very real threat of a centralised, privileged mode of operation. Microelectronic technology is now at the stage from which the 'information society' could evolve into either of these models. The term 'evolve' is used here because it is doubtful whether governments would manage to comprehend the possible changes and would therefore fail to clearly define the required role of technology and the criteria under which information systems should develop. The result of this could be the piecemeal acquistion of such systems which, inevitably, would reflect the motivation of the designers and would maintain the status quo of the financiers.

5.3.1 Computer-Assisted Coordination

The only example of one nation attempting to fully computerise the operation of its entire economy occured in Chile during the period of 1972-73, under the Allende government.† An effort was made by a team headed by the cybernetics expert Stafford Beer to produce a real-time nerve centre that could monitor, and to some extent coordinate, the workings of the Chilean economy. By 1973, 40% of the nation's activities were linked to the computer system, although it is not clear to what level the system was operational. The object of the CYBERSYN project was to

> "1) rapidly increase the efficiency of the nationalised sectors, 2) strengthen the economy against the CIA financed right wing of Chilean society and 3) allow for the development of greatly increased popular participation in the management of society. . . The problem was to organise prediction so that decisions could be made at the most appropriate level, be it shopfloor, national planning or some level in between." (Athanasiou 1980).

† A more detailed description is given in Beer (1975).

The structure envisaged by Beer was one of hierarchical information flow and, to this end, a computer network was established throughout the nation with 'Operations Rooms' built at all key sites – (only one Ops Room was actually completed). Information was displayed primarily in the form of graphs, block diagrams or flow charts, an essential feature of which was the ability to successfully subdivide the displays so that more data became available. In this way a national organisation wishing to look into steel production for example, could examine graphs depicting its progress and, if required, these could be subdivided either into different grades of steel or regional production. A steel plant manager could use the same information to survey the overall working of his or her factory and a 'foreman' could see exactly what each worker was doing. The information network bore similarities to the human nervous system; at each level action could be controlled and monitored but if things began to malfunction, a higher level could take over and make appropriate decisions. The task of the technology was to filter the data moving to the top of the hierachy, so that only important information reached the national planners. For example, a fall in production levels, over one monthly period, would be brought to the attention of the factory managers in that industrial sector. Over two or three months, an area organiser would be consulted and, after perhaps six months of poor performance, it would warrant the attention of some government official. As Beer pointed out, when describing his experiences with CYBERSYN:

> "One of the main issues identified was the issue of autonomy, or participation, or perhaps I just mean liberty, for whatever viable system. Then this means that there ought to be a computable function setting the degree of centralisation consistent with effectiveness and with freedom at every level of recursion."
> (Beer 1975).

Recursion is a cybernetic term meaning, in this context, each part of the hierarchy. What Beer wanted was a system that gave as much local autonomy as possible whilst retaining effective global coordination. It is important to understand that CYBERSYN was intended to *coordinate* activity not *control* it. This is a crucial distinction and one that is rarely understood by designers of information systems.

Unfortunately, the results of Beer's designs were never put to the test; initially work was hindered by a US economic blockade and the Allende government was later overthrown in a military coup. Inevitably, what was considered coordination by one government was interpreted as control by the next. The present fate of CYBERSYN is not known. A further aspect of Beer's national information structure was a planning system which he called 'futures'. In effect, this was an 'expert system' as it endeavoured to simulate and predict such economic variables as employment, inflation, borrowing requirement and so on. It enabled national planners to investigate the likely outcome of activities such as decreasing the interest rates or increasing government investment. By having to update statistics on the economy, CYBERSYN could counteract the secondary effects so often present in financial planning. In Britain, important data such as that outlined above, is always two or three months out of date, because of the primitive way the information is collected. The result of this is that the government is working with a picture of the economy that is no longer correct and it is therefore not surprising that the action taken is so often inappropriate.

This is the same effect that one encounters when taking a shower. If it becomes too hot you turn the temperature down but, because it takes a long time for this action to have any result, you often turn the controller too far and, before long, you are having a cold shower. By repeating this action, the shower would oscillate between hot and cold; the best way to control this process would be to have up to date information on the temperature of the water as it works its way through the system. This is essentially what Beer wished for the Chilean economy. By efficient information flow in the 'now' sector, the 'futures' program would at least be able to work with the right data.

Perhaps the greatest criticism of CYBERSYN is that the distinction between coordination and control was too nebulous. Was it a means of producing an efficient decentralised nation or a 'sinister tool of authoritarian manipulation'? Beer undoubtedly believed that it was the former, although it is not clear what safeguards could be incorporated to protect the community from the latter. Another interesting facet of the Chilean experiment is that it illustrates the difference between information systems which enhance local autonomy and those which encourage decision making participation. CYBERSYN was designed so as to provide as much control as possible to those who were immediately affected. In the interests of efficient coordination, however, a hierarchy existed which allowed important issues to filter up to the level at which they would best be dealt with. This does not mean that units lower down the structure can participate in these more complex decisions. In the last section, on systems analysis, it was emphasised that Management Information Systems could be designed so that large numbers of people could take part in the decision making process, in many instances at the cost of tighter control over the system's operation. In other words, a MIS can encourage participation but it may be to the detriment of local autonomy. It should be possible to develop systems that incorporate both of these features although this is difficult to visualise since in order to make decisions one must be informed, and to have information one must monitor the activity of others. By contrast, autonomy means making decisions that affect oneself; not allowing others to become involved with, or even know of, one's everyday plans and performance.

In many ways this is the same problem that exists with privacy and public knowledge. Personal data must be protected against public misuse, and public information should be available to all. Perhaps one possible solution to this dilemma might be to use the new programming language, Ada, as a model because this language incorporates self-contained program *modules*, which have free information flow within them, whilst only data that are defined to be in a 'window' can be seen from the rest of the program. That is to say, within a structure there are individual units, inside which it could be said that there is total participation, and yet the autonomy of each unit is protected by its ability to define what the rest of the structure has access to.

5.3.2 Public Videotex

Since Beer's experiments in Chile, no similar comprehensive information systems have been proposed. Interest has grown, however, around videotex or viewdata and teletext, for as Godfrey Boyle of the Open University Alternative Technology group explains:

> "There is no reason why the kind of information which Beer planned to make available on his Chilean system could not equally easily be made available on the Viewdata network. Easy-to-understand graphical and numerical displays of the current state, and possible future states, of the United Kingdom economy could be accessed on demand. Citizens, having considered the issues, could then register their votes electronically on what to do." (Boyle 1980).

Videotex can bring information to the community, and it can also communicate the opinions of individuals to central bodies. In Chapter 3, a detailed assessment of public Videotex systems was offered and it is perhaps worthwhile summarising the features necessary before such systems can be considered convivial.

Firstly there is the question of cost; the British system, Prestel is at present expensive whilst, on the other hand, nations such as France have opted to offer their telecommunication equipment without charge; between these two extremes there are a number of marketing approaches. Of more importance than individual cost will be the extent to which libraries, schools and other public centres make Prestel available. To assist the development of an orderly information system British Telecom have decided to license a number of information providers, who are responsible for the data. A better approach might be to encourage members of the public to participate in the system. In this way, videotex would reflect more the two-way communications of the telephone rather than that of the television where 99.9% of the population have no say in nor contribution to the medium apart from paying for it.

To enhance participation, the mailbox facility whereby pages of information can be transferred between individuals, should be central to the scheme even though this would necessitate more sophisticated user equipment. A viable public information system could be made up of individual users, small organisations, local institutions, regional groups and national enterprises. Within the operation of any electronic information service there must be built-in protections for the right to privacy of every member of the public. This can only be effectively accomplished with the aid of statutory data protection legislation.

At the national level, government must endeavour to keep its own information service up to date, in that the data 'published' should be correct and complete. A 'freedom of information act' in Britain may be required to enforce this.

Other nations have begun to realise that by keeping the public well informed, greater credibility can be attached to government action. As well as the government, other national organisations who would profit from more efficient information technology include advertsiers, consumer protectors, travel agents etc. A further nationwide application was considered by Lord Avebury:

> "That there is the technology available for computer based welfare benefits information systems applied to the complex mass of roles in the UK has been demonstrated long ago, and it has also been shown that with the aid of these systems, many people not now receiving the benefits to which they are entitled would be alerted to their rights."† (Avebury 1978).

At the regional level Prestel, or its equivalent, will be of most use as an information store for locally based groups and a community notice board. A communicative system would avail itself of this facility far more than one in which information only flows in one direction. If Videotex is to assume the role of a traditional library it must be just as appropriate; this can only be achieved if the internal structure and mode of operation are generally understood.

The indexing method must be straightforward, such as that used by Prestel. It must also be comprehensive in terms of finding *all* relevant pages when asked, and flexible in its ability to allow users to browse or 'laterally' search through the available material. If, as seems likely with the French scheme, a variety of data bases are to be held on the same telecommunication system, different indexing methods will be developed and demonstrated. Only through extensive trials will the most appropriate public information system be designed.

Of the many uses to which Prestel has already been applied, it is difficult to differentiate between those which will become permanent features and the ones which will prove to have been only a novelty. The popularity of mail order shopping might indicate that this facet of videotex will remain and yet probably the biggest growth area might be in closed user groups, where physically distant elements of some company or institution would employ the standard public system, in order to collate and communicate information. A closed user group under Prestel consists of a regional organisation exercising control over a number of pages only accessible to its own members. This access is sometimes at a high cost if the organisation considers its information valuable. Prestel, like CYBERSYN, will thus be primarily a technology for coordination-an increasingly important function in any industrial or post-industrial society.

When considering the role of public information technology and the development of an appropriate structure, it must always be remembered that not every member of society will wish to or be able to make use of it. Even if the equipment is free and telephones are installed in every home, there will still be people who have no use for the service, and for many years this group might be the majority of the population. The essence of convivial or appropriate technology

† This possibility is discussed at length by Adler (1975).

is not that it must be used by everyone but that it could be, if people wish it. Public knowledge is obtained from a variety of media, of which Videotex is an isolated example. Society must decide whether others forms of media, threatened by these new techniques, should be given economic protection to ensure their survival.

5.3.3 Personal Computers

Although a number of individuals have bought microcomputers for their own use, the term 'personal computer' has become recognised as meaning a home based piece of equipment. The popularity of this type of computer is witnessed by the increasing volume of magazines and books aimed at these users. Publications range from those dealing with the electronics angle, through the entire micro-computer field to the small business system. There is no shortage of information and equipment and so for those who want one, a small computer can be obtained for the price of a small car.

One of the most important functions of a home based machine would be to link it to a domestic network (when they become available) thereby turning the stand-alone micro into just one element of a large information system. Electronic mail and videotex services will increase the usefulness of this home unit. For people concerned with organising small businesses or institutions the micro-computer becomes a straightforward aid. The type of application mentioned in 'Systems Analysis' is equally applicable here. With a popular microcomputer, the large number of programs available provide all manner of business functions. These are generally written in BASIC and can be modified by anyone familiar with this essentially simple language. This would help provide the flexibility essential in any organisational environment. As well as businesses, any group working on a join venture may profit from the use of a microcomputer to plan regular activities or monitor finance.

On a truly personal basis, the microcomputer can have a number of uses, including keeping a diary, noting which bills are paid or outstanding and even cataloguing one's record collection. In addition, and perhaps of more practical benefit, the small computer can function as a word-processor. Although the injudicious use of word-processors has been one of the earliest examples of microelectronics causing unemployment, their use as a personal text editor and typewriter can have enormous advantages. The only equipment needed for this use is a small microcomputer with a floppy disc unit for storage and a good quality printer. The software for the text organisation can either be developed or bought. Word-processors must favourably affect productivity because their use saves considerable time, effort and paper.

Entertainment

It is doubtful whether any of the applications just mentioned can be considered of great social benefit in a macroscopic sense. What is clear is that they are both useful and interesting. Microelectronics has a more frivolous aspect, it is after all, an elaborate construction kit which will occupy many people's attention by the sheer fascination of its intricacies. Programming, as has already been noted, is a very entertaining and rewarding activity, especially if it is done as a hobby rather than a chore. No matter what the end product, the exploration of the capabilities of a computer is both appealing and stimulating.

People who take up programming as a career rarely become bored writing software, even after several years of work. There is, within all of us, a fascination for machines that are capable of outstripping the human scale. The very quick and the very small are features of the micro and understandably, this has captured the imagination of many people. Computer games of all shapes and sizes have been invented in the last few years and have provided considerable amusement. The attraction of these machines lies in their sophistication and the genuine skill needed to play them.

There are, as previously mentioned, an alarming number of instances in which admiration for the technology has developed into something akin to addiction. This is a very serious matter, particularly as society becomes more technical. On the other hand, there are people who are intimidated by and suspicious of computer equipment and will have nothing at all to do with it. In extreme cases this can become virtual 'microphobia'; again, this is a source of concern for the futute.

The 'answer' to these extremes must lie, as solutions often do, in education – both formally in the school and college and also by general social interaction. The first objective must be to de-mystify the micro, explain how it works, what it can or cannot do, in order to produce healthy informed scepticism. Secondly, the role of microelectronics within the wider social setting should be continually emphasised in order that technology can be associated with clearly understood human attributes and activities. Finally the technology must be used in such a way as to increase both familiarity and understanding. The more entertaining the technology, the more people will use it. This will help cement the bond of its interaction to existing social structures.

5.4 MONITORING AND CONTROL – PROGRAMMABLE SYSTEMS

It would appear that the main impact of microelectronics and telecommunications will be felt in the data processing and information handling areas of domestic, commercial and industrial application. The main changes, greatest dangers and potential benefits of the 'new technology' are due to its innovatory structure. There are, nevertheless, other fields in which the micro has a substantial part to play and in this section we will consider its role in the development of programmable controllers and monitors. Programmable because the alternative, an embedded system – where the micro is merely obeying a permanent sequence of instructions

– gives the user no structural control over the equipment. Whether such applications are 'socially motivated' depends not on the internal micro but on the external functions of the tool itself. This is true to a certain extent of any control system but at least if it is programmable the user has some design influence over its operation.

For equipment to contain a programmable micro it must contain a *port* or *interface*† to which a VDU can be attached. This adds to the cost and complexity of the system and is unwarranted in many controllers and monitors. The fuel system in a car can be made more efficient by micro control but there is no need for the driver to reprogram this operation. Other systems, however, justify user involvement; for example with a domestic central heating controller a suitable interface to a personal computer would allow structural changes to be made, such as the addition of an extra radiator.

5.4.1 Environmental Monitors

One type of equipment which is an obvious advantage in advanced industrial nations is the environmental monitor which can continually report pollution levels. The Minos system for controlling mines (Chapter 3) demonstrates the increased safety that can be achieved by close computer control over atmospheric sensors. Pollution observers all around the world now have to contend with the most sophisticated forms of waste, and they need cheap computing power to undertake the accurate analysis required. Complicated systems would also be of great value in the monitoring of energy usage: at the beginning of the chapter it was explained how numerical computer work can help in the design of efficient heating systems. As important is the accurate monitoring of equipment that is already in operation.

Consider the experience of one firm with a large energy outlay and many buildings to heat. Sainsburys, the London based chain store, has 244 branches of which 199 are supermarkets. Their fuel bill for the financial year 1978-79 was over £7 million. This firm was already concious of its energy expenditure and had initiated many operating changes in order to increase thermal efficiency when they considered close automatic monitoring in an attempt to reduce their fuel bill by over £1 million. One of their first measures was to introduce a monitor/controller for the electrical load in their main office:

> "Costing £17,000 the 'Enertrol' system yielded savings in electricity worth £13,000 a year over the first year of operation.
>   Essentially the system continuously monitors electrical load and predicts likely demand. If the forecast shows that the set maximum demand will be exceeded then loads are programmed to be switched off." (*Energy Management* August 1980).

---

† An interface is a piece of equipment or logic which allows computers to be linked either together or to other equipment, so that information can pass between them.

Sainsburys are now considering a far more ambitious scheme based on a distributed system. Initially, five branches (later to be expanded to 80 if the trial is successful) will be equipped with stand-alone computers to monitor heating, lighting and ventilation levels, as well as test for faults in refrigerators. These control units will be programmed to work independently and will endeavour to reduce fuel consumption. The system is distributed because the local computers automatically 'report' to a central machine using standard telephone lines. This central computer monitors the satellites and hence overall control of the operating criteria can be maintained and alterations made in response to incoming data. The essence of this scheme, if it works correctly, is that the computers and operators will become more efficient the longer the equipment is used. How much control will rest with the local users, as opposed to the central planners, is not clear, but obviously a scheme like this could be structured so that the user can direct the immediate system whilst obtaining operational advice from an overall monitor.

In domestic energy matters, a small scale monitoring system can also be cost effective and useful. A normal house has a variety of rooms used for different functions which should ideally be at different temperatures at different times of the day. There are already microprocessor controlled central heating systems which offer the user this type of service. All rooms would have a thermostat and the desired temperature can be altered from a central controller. By reducing fuel consumption this equipment can pay for itself in under two years! A simple domestic system would have a relatively straightforward design and a comprehensive control panel would alleviate the need for the micro at the heart of the control to be programmable. In large complexes it would be beneficial to allow the system to be restructured to meet physical and operational changes, this would necessitate having some programming expertise or, at least, 'program generating' software.

If buildings contain such progressive features as solar panels, heat pumps, thermal storage and possibly battery electronic storage, data must be continuously obtained so that long term energy strategies can be developed. A thermal store, where one hopes to hold enough 'summer' heat to last through the winter, is a very inert system and does not easily react to short term changes. In order to monitor all the important parameters in such an overall energy system, a number of isolated meters could be employed and rule of thumb methods used to control the system. A microcomputer will not take over this work but it could be an invaluable tool. It can monitor as many devices as required and, more importantly, it will keep a complete history of all such readings. In thermal systems, the trends are more important than absolute readings, and it is virtually impossible for anyone to handle more than six or seven inter-dependent variables. The microcomputer can manage this with ease and can even be designed so that overall control remains with the individual responsible.

Although there are some exclusively monitoring applications, most systems, such as those above, contain an element of control. This implies that the operation of the total system is affected by computer decisions which are based upon monitored information. For example, if a room is too cold the heating is turned up or, if the atmospheric conditions are right, solar water heating is activated. One way of distinguishing between monitoring and control is to compare open and closed systems. An open loop needs somebody to interpret monitored measurements in order to initiate control actions. A closed loop needs no human intervention because the computer can make its own decisions based upon the data. A combination of these methods, which in many cases is the most appropriate, is where the computer operates in a closed loop fashion for the minute by minute control, but the user is completely in charge of the strategic decisions the system is making. In this way, the user remains at the centre of the system's operation but does not have to spend the entire time controlling its every action.

To describe in detail how monitoring and control equipment is linked to a microcomputer one should consider, at some length, a particular application which is perhaps destined to have a considerable significance in an oil scarce world.

5.4.2 Fermentation Control
It has been argued that when fossil fuel supplies are economically exhausted, the bulk of the world's chemical requirements will have to be satisfied by microbial fermentation of plant-derived carbohydrates. As a result, fermentation performance and control is likely to become increasingly important through the remainder of this decade and the next. Even renowned groups such as the Advisory Council for Applied Research and Development, a working party of the Advisory Board of the Research Councils, and the Royal Society, reported in 1980 that:

> "We envisage biotechnology – the application of biological organisms, systems or processes to manufacturing and service industries – creating wholly novel industries, with low fossil energy demands, which will be of key importance to the world economy in the next century."

The popular view of micro-organism activities is usually depicted in terms of the standard methane production, but this is not the only case where fermentation technology is employed to produce industrially useful products, such as acetone and butanol. With all types of biotechnological processes, computers are finding themselves in increasing demand:

> "For example, computers are already having an impact on research into fermentation processes. Process control computers are being used in fermentation pilot plant and look set to play an increasingly important part in the fermentation industry. This development has been aided by numerous studies using computers in the investigation and control of microbial production processes." (Tongue 1980).

The oldest example of fermentation must be the action of yeast on sugar to form alcohol; home brewing requires no computer control but the large production plants in Brazil do. Brazil is currently the world's largest producer of alcohol, following an ambitious oil saving programme that will lead to the nation's road traffic running on gasohol, a mixture of 80% petrol and 20% alcohol. Penicillin, formed by a fungal growth, is another instance of a microbial reaction which has unquestionably been of social benefit and which lends itself to a computer controlled production process.

Optimising Production

"There are two ways in which the productivity of an industrial fermentation may be enhanced; (a) by mutation and selection for high-yielding strains, that is to say by genetic manipulation, and (b) by optimising the chemical and physical environment of the fermenter during the fermentation process." (Kell 1980).

The scope of the possible improvements is illustrated by considering the commercial fermentation of penicillin G. In the last 35 years the yield of this process has improved 25,000 times! This is not the end of the story for, as has been shown that in recent industrial trials only 60% of the glucose (the starting point for fermentation) is turned into penicillin.

"The actual yield of penicillin from glucose is an order of magnitude from the theoretical value and there is room for substantial improvement." (Cooney 1979).

Leaving aside the possibility of genetic engineering, which has a number of questionable facets, one is left with a natural process to manipulate. It has been understood for a long time that, by controlling the level of pH in the fermentation environment, yields can be dramatically improved. This is usually achieved by immersing a glass electrode into the solution which then registers hydrogen ions (or pH) and activates a pump if the desired set point is not reached. The pumped solution will have a known acid or base strength. With experimental work, the electrode is usually connected to a chart recorder which gives a permanent description of fermentor behaviour.

The pH level is not the only significant factor. Oxygen is another followed by calcium, potassium, sodium, chloride, bromide, silver, sulphur, fluoride, lead, copper and dissolved gases such as carbon dioxide, sulphur dioxide, nitrogen trioxide and ammonia, all of which can be measured electronically. Enzymes are critical in many fermentations, and physical conditions, such as temperature and pressure, are always important.

Research would indicate that by close control (tolerance ± 0.5%), all these ion concentrations would greatly increase both the yield and product range, for the environment not only affects the yield of the process, but also the direction in which it moves. The technical problem is how to link all these monitors and controllers together in a single operating unit.

Computers transfer signals to other equipment via a *bus*, which is a collection of wires down which electrical messages are sent in a designed sequence. If some peripheral device has the facility to translate these messages it can also communicate with the computer. Microcomputers use a number of buses, all of which have particular operating characteristics which make them suitable for certain tasks. The most common means of linking a microcomputer to a peripheral, such as a line printer, is by the RS232 interface; within the computer the S100 bus is the most popular model used for communications between the processor, the memory and the disc drive. With both the RS232 and S100 speed of operation is very important, because they are concerned with moving information around the computer system. When the application is one of piecing together various types of laboratory or industrial equipment with a microcomputer, speed is less important and ease of use becomes the central criterion. One means of acquiring this kind of system is to use the standard IEEE-488 bus.

Fermentation Control Apparatus

The conventional fermentation controller has a single glass electrode which registers pH and is linked first to a voltmeter and then either to a chart recorder or pump activator. If 15 or more ion-selective electrodes are to be employed then this conventional method would require the same number of accurate and expensive voltmeters. A more efficient system has only one voltmeter and a *scanner* which will quickly look at all the electrodes in turn and feed each reading to the voltmeter. This introduces the new problem of how to keep track of what is going on, both in terms of logging the performance and activating the appropriate pumps. With 15 ions being monitored 15 pumps are required to maintain control over each ion concentration. The complexity of a system such as this necessitates computer assistance because it is beyond the capability of a human operator.

Fig. 5.2 illustrates a complete set of apparatus, developed at the University of Wales, Aberystwyth, based on a microcomputer and which uses the IEEE-bus to coordinate the necessary devices. The equipment consists of:

1. Microcomputer with keyboard and screen.
2. Chart recorder.
3. Floppy disc unit.
4. Line printer.
5. Digital voltmeter.
6. Scanner.
7. Pump housing.

The electrodes emit an analogue signal of between 0 and 2 volts. The scanner forwards this reading to the voltmeter which then outputs a digital reading onto the bus. These operations are under the control of the microcomputer which, amongst other things, selects which electrode is to be read. From the voltage reading, the computer, using specially written software, calculates the ionic concentrations in the fermentor vessel and will then undertake a number of functions:

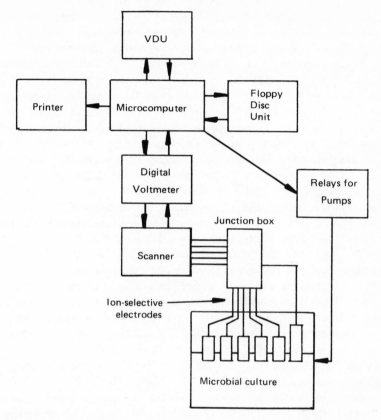

Fig. 5.2 – Diagrammatic representation of a computer controlled fermentation system.

(i) Keeps an updated record on the VDU screen.

(ii) Prints out on the line printer, at intervals the state of the fermentor and any action taken.

(iii) Keeps a record of the experiment process run on floppy discs.

(iv) Gives chart recorder readings for up to twelve electrodes – this is the traditional medium and is still required by many experimenters; in the future a graphic VDU might well replace it.

(v) If any ionic concentration has drifted beyond tolerance, the appropriate pump can be instructed to add a measured amount of ion solution.

All these tasks are instigated via the IEEE-bus and require only simply programming. In addition to the usual sensors, there would normally be thermo-couples to register temperature and an on/off heater activated by the bus. The software needed to run the rig is straightforward, the only difficulty is that the electrodes are not perfectly selective. Although a pH electrode will react sensitively to hydrogen ions it will also, to a greater or lesser extent, register changes in other ions such as potassium. This can be taken into account in the programs but it does lead to some complications.

The advantages of using this type of computer controlled equipment are many. Primarily it makes possible what would otherwise be extremely difficult. Secondly, for experimental purposes it is a thousand times more accurate than the non-computer method and provides a more comprehensive record which can be analysed later. The cost of the computer equipment is negligible in comparison with the expense of the fermentor vessel. Ultimately, the benefit of the system rests in its ability to produce valuable chemicals from renewable resources, on a small scale basis. Fermentation is a most appropriate technology.

The role of the computer in this type of experiment is essentially one of an information controller; it organises the vacillation of data from instrument to instrument, and from the system as a whole to the user. It facilitates instant read outs on the VDU, records of trends on the chart recorder, written accounts on the line printer and a permanent description of the entire proceedings on the disc unit. The user must arrange the system in terms of electrode choice and desired ionic concentrations and then leave the minute by minute control to the microcomputer. This is not a case of a machine replacing a human, for without the micro this type of fermentor would be impossible.

Bioelectronics, the joining together of biotechnology and microelectronics, is a growing and important area, which will become tomorrow's 'new technology'. For example, we can develop effective pollution controllers capable of filtering low concentration toxics from the atmosphere. Not only will biotechnology be at the centre of many chemical processes it will also make them non-pollutant, or at least substantially cleaner than they are at present. How fast our economy moves towards these ends depends upon many factors, not least of which is the availability of cheap and easy methods of amalgamating individual instruments into viable and comprehensive systems. By using standard buses, control systems can be constructed (like a child's Lego set) and the whole process can be activated by some reasonably straightforward software. The IEEE-488 is by no means an ideal bus; for instance it should never be used to link devices that need a fast data transfer rate, such as the CPU and disc unit. But equipment that is IEEE compatible is guaranteed to be bus controllable.

Industrial processes must be made to work as efficiently and safely as possible and be pollution free. Computer control can fulfil such specifications whilst furnishing the user with more flexible equipment, but whether or not it will, returns us to the question of the society's demands on technology and the motivation and expectations of the designers and financiers of tomorrow's tools.

5.5 OVERVIEW

Whether a few isolated examples of socially beneficial applications can make a whole technology appear appropriate is debatable. The optimist's approach would probably be to proclaim microelectronics as a salutary agent, based on some of its more obviously useful aspects. However, it is similarly misleading to take the pessimist's view and use a few socially harmful applications to brand microelectronics as either oppressive or inhumane.

If one looks at the evolution of the micro from the large computers in the 1960s and 70s then a rather jaundiced view may be excused. Mainframe data processing computers remained the province of large institutions and multi-national companies, they were simply not available to other people. Meanwhile, the micro was being nurtured by the military for weapons guidance and the early detection of enemy attack. To take the most favourable view, this sophisticated hardware can be beneficial to the community at large for its deterrent value alone, its major contribution being one of non-usage!

Although the micro grew away from a purely military application, it is still seen as a technology of the establishment. The possible disappearance of our privacy, jobs and newspapers is a sacrifice to state security, productivity and efficiency, and not of immediate benefit to the individuals actually affected by these changes. To counter this, or least to justify it more fully, independent assessment, government legislation and community based schemes are required. Even in education the innocent use of new technological aids could have a dramatic effect upon the type of learning which takes place and the skills with which tomorrow's workforce will be equipped. The phrase 'new technology' has been used to describe the micro and certainly, in terms of the hardware, a chip is a relatively new phenomenon. Its application area is, however, rarely a fundamental one. The implementation of computer technology in machinery control, numerical analysis, teaching aids, information transfer, facsimile communication, word-processing and data storage has influenced but not initiated the process, because all these activities have, in one way or another, preceded the micro. Even the inherent concepts of a computer are not significantly new, for the nineteenth century witnessed the description of a machine which is still an adequate model of a modern computer. The important factor is that of the scale of its application.

To understand the role of the micro, one must first appreciate the place of technology in society, and have criteria by which particular tools or instruments may be assessed. 'Appropriateness' is a name that has been given to any technology that satisfies certain conditions in terms of its effects upon the community and environment. The microchip, whether it be used as a processor, a memory or for some specialised purpose, is the raw material of microcomputer technology. It has no direct application other than its role as building block for other technologies. The programmable microchip fulfills most of the criteria for appropriateness and bears the hallmark (in Illich's term) of a convivial tool. It will only become inappropriate when applied to systems, tools and aids which do not provide an obvious social and environmental advantage.

Apart from a quite simple embedded system, LSI technology is used in a variety of devices all of which can be broadly described as a computer. That is, they take in data, manipulate it according to some memorised set of instructions, store it where necessary and output information when required. In general, the set of instructions can be changed, i.e. the computer is programmable. This description is equally true of small personal computers and the largest IBM mainframe, because the function of any computer is to process information. This may either be presented in large volumes, as in an 'information system', or the processing might be quite complex, as in numerical work. The computer can keep people 'informed' or it can drive other equipment, as in process control. Essentially, all these tasks are the same, and some general observations about all micro-based equipment can be made:

1. They aid information analysis, retrieval and distribution.
2. They reduce the energy and materials requirement, and are non-pollutant.
3. They lend an air of authority to the emanating information which reflects more upon the sophistication of the technology than the accuracy of the data.
4. They can store all manner of data, including the irrelevant, inaccurate and harmful. There is no constraint upon information storage.

Notwithstanding the significance of the final two points, the microchip can render control equipment more efficient and clean, and information systems more effective. Distributed decision making and increased public knowledge could be the consequence of new technology, which might result in the establishment of more appropriate industrial and chemical processes. Alternatively, oppressive state control, mass unemployment and even larger manufacturing units are possible threats. The microchip can be misused (indeed, its own assembly bears more than a taint of exploitation) but 'misuse' it would be, for structurally the microchip is an appropriate technology.

References and Reports

REFERENCES

Ackoff, R. L. (1978), From information to control. *Human side of information processing*, ed. Bjorn-Andersen, North-Holland Publishing Company.

Adler, M. and D. du Feu. (1975), A computer based welfare benefits information system, *The Inverclyde Project*, UK Scientific Section IBM.

Alcock, D. (1977), *Illustrating Basic*, Cambridge University Press.

Ashman, P. (1979), Report from the workshop on police and national security records, *Computers, Records and the Right to Privacy*, ed. P. Hewitt, Input Two-Nine.

Athanasiou, T. (1980), The liberty machine, *Undercurrents* 38.

Avebury, Lord. (1978), *The impact of computers on society seen from the western viewpoint*, DIGICO publications.

Babbage, C. (1837), *On the mathematical power of the calculating machine*, Reprint in Randall (1973).

Babbage, C. (1864), *Passage from the life of a philosopher*, Longman, Reprinted by Augustus M. Kelly, New York.

Barron, I. M. (1978), The future of computer technology, *Information technology*, ed. J. Moneta.

Barron, I. M. and Curnow, R. (1979), *The future with microelectronics*, Francis Pinter.

Beer, S. (1975), *Platform for change*, Wiley.

Belden, T. G. and Belden, M. R. (1962), *The lengthening shadow: the life of Thomas J. Watson*, Boston.

Birnbaum, R. (1978), *Health hazards of visual display units*, Occupational Health, London School of Hygeine and Tropical Medicine.

Bodington, S. (1974), *Computers and socialism*, Spokesman Books.

Boyle, G. (1980), *Private Communication*, Alternative Technology Group of the Open University.

Braverman, H. (1974), *Labor and Monopoly Capital*, Monthly Review Press.

Bunyan, T. (1979), Police and national security records, see Ashman (1979).

Colin, A. J. T. (1980), *Fundamentals of Computer Science*, Macmillan Computer Science Series.

Cooney, C. L. (1979), *Process Biochemistry*.

Davis, W. S. and McCormack, A. (1979), *The information age*, Addison-Wesley.

Dickson, D. (1974), *Alternative technology and the politics of technical change*, Fontana.

Dockerty, P. (1979), *User participation in and influence on systems design in Norway and Sweden in the light of union involvement, new legislation and joint agreements*, See Ackoff (1978).

Dubbey, J. M. (1977), Babbage, Peacock and modern algebra, *Historia Mathematica*, **Vol 4**.

Evans, C. (1979a), *The mighty micro*, Victor Gollancz Ltd.

Evans, C. (1979b), *New scientist*.

Feickert, D. (1979), Of mice and minos. *Computing Europe*.

Flad, J. P. (1958), L'horloge à calcul de l'astronome W. Schickard semble avoir été la première machine à calcul à engrenages propre aux 4 operations, *Chiffres*, **Vol 1**.

Foy, G. (1980), Private Communication. *Microprocessors for a parallel culture*.

Freeman, C. (1979), Government policies for industrial innovation, *The Ninth J. B. Bernal Lecture, Birkbeck College*, See also Senker (1979).

Freese, J. (1978), *The Swedish data act*, Transnational data regulations, Online, England.

Frobl, F., Heinrichs, J. and Kreye, O. (1980), *The New International Division of Labour*, Cambridge University Press.

Garret, J. (1980), *Undercurrents* **40**.

Goldstine, H. H. (1972), *The computer from Pascal to Von Neumann*, Princeton University Press.

Good, I. J. (1970), Some future social repercussions of computers, *International Journal for Environmental Studies*, **Vol 1**.

Gosling, W. (1978), *Microcircuits, society and education*, Occasional paper No 8, Council for educational technology for the United Kingdom.

Hobsbawn, E. J. and Rude, G. (1969), *Captain Swing*, Lawrence and Wishort, London.

Hoffman, (1980), *Computers and Privacy in the next decade*, Academic.

Hooper, R. (1980), *The Guardian-Futures*, April 24th.

Hunt, R. and Shelley, J. (1979), *Computers and Commonsense*, Prentice Hall.

Illich, I. (1973), *Tools for convivialty*, Fontana.

Jenkins, C. and Sherman, B. (1979), *The collapse of work*, Methuen.

Kell, D. B. (1980), The role of ion-selective electrodes in improving fermentation yields, *Process Biochemistry*.

Kirkham, J. and Dye, J. R. (1980), *The scheduling of production in a small firm using a micro system*, Online, England.

Land, F. F. (1979), *The changing face of computer education,* Selected Essays in Contemporary Computing, ed. A. Simpson, Input Two-Nine.

Laver, F. J. M. (1974), Information, engineering and society, *The Ninth Maurice Lubbock Memorial Lecture.*

Laver, M. (1976), *Introducing Computers,* HMSO.

Lavington, S. (1980), *Early British computers,* Manchester University Press.

McRobie, G. (1975), *An approach for appropriate technologies,* Lectures on socially appropriate technology, ed. R. J. Congdon, CICA, Netherlands, Also available as: *Introduction to appropriate technology – Towards a simpler life style,* Rodale Press, 1977.

McLuhan, M. (1964), *Understanding media,* Sphere Books.

Meek, B. L. and Fairthorne, S. (1977), *Using Computers,* Ellis Horwood.

Meek, B. L. and Heath, P. (1980), *Guide to Good Programming Practice,* Ellis Horwood.

Menninger, K. (1969), *Number words and number systems: A cultural history of number,* MIT Press.

Michie, D. (1980), *Expert systems in the micro-electronic age,* Edinburgh University Press.

Moore, L. (1980), *Foundations of programming with Pascal,* Ellis Horwood.

Morrison, P. (1961), *Charles Babbage and his calculating engines,* Dover Publications.

Morton, J., Barnard, P., Hammond, N. and Long, J. B. (1979), Interacting with the computer: a framework, *Teleinformatics – Report of joint project: MRC Applied Psychology Unit,* Cambridge and IBM Peterlee.

Moseley, M. (1964), *Irascible genius: A life of Charles Baggabe, Inventer,* Hutchinson.

Mowshowitz, A. (1977), *Inside information,* Addison-Wesley.

Nora, S. and Minc, A. (1978), *L'Informatisation de la société,* la documentation Francaise. Also available as *The Computerisation of Society,* MIT Press, 1980.

Page, A. (1980), Blueprint or Greentown? *Undercurrents* **42.**

Phillips, C. A. (1978), Report from committee on data systems languages. *Sigplan Notices, History of programming conference.*

Pyle, I. C. (1979), Proceedings of the IRONMAN language seminar, *University of York Report.*

Randall, B. (1973), *The origins of digital computers: Selective papers,* Springer-Verlang.

Rothwell, R. and Zegfeld, W. (1980), *Technical change and unemployment,* Francis Pinter.

Rohl, J. S. (1977), *Programming in Fortran,* Manchester University Press.

Sammett, J. E. (1969), *Programming languages: history and fundamentals,* Prentice Hall.

Schumacher, E. F. (1974), *Small is beautiful,* Abacus.

Seidenberg, A. (1960), *The diffusion of counting practices,* University of California Publications in Mathematics.

Senker, P. (1979), Social implications of automation, *The Industrial Robot.*

Shannon, C. (1938), A symbolic analysis of relay and switching circuits, *Trans. Amer. Inst. Eng.* Vol 57.

Simmons, G. L. (1979), *Introducing microprocessors,* NCC.

Sleigh, J., Boatwright, B., Irwin, P. and Stangon, R. (1979), *The manpower implications of micro-electronic technology,* HMSO.

Smith, T. M. (1970), Some perspectives on the early history of computers, *Perspectives on the computer revolution,* ed. Z. W. Pylyshyn, Prentice Hall.

Stewart, T. F. M. (1977), *An ergonomic checklist,* Loughborough University, UK.

Stokes, A. V. (1979), Design of future networks, *Selective Essays in Contemporary Computing,* Input Two-Nine.

Stonier, T. (1979a), The impact of the micro-processor on society – the future of employment, *Science in society project,* Malvern College.

Stonier, T. (1979b), The third industrial revolution, microprocessors and robots, *IMF Central Committee Meeting,* Vienna.

Sutton, C. (1979), Taking the mystery out of the micro, *New Scientist,* 540-542.

Thomas, M. I. (1970), *The Luddites,* David and Chales Deron.

Toffler, A. (1980), *The third wave,* Collins.

Tongue, C. (1980), The uncertain romance of the bug and the chip, *Computing.*

Trevelyan, G. M. (1946) *English social history: a survey of six centuries,* Longman.

Tropp, H. S. (1978), Generation minus one – the bell labs relay computers, *Information Technology,* ed. J. Moneta.

Uhlig, R. P., Farber, D. J. and Bair, J. H. (1979), *The office of the future,* Monograph series of the international council for computer communications, North-Holland.

Usher, A. P. (1954), *A history of mechanical invention, 2nd revised edition,* Cambridge, Mass: Harvard University Press.

Von Neumann, J. (1948), The general and logical theory of automata, *Symposium lecture Pasadeng, Collective works* Vol 5.

Von Neumann, J. (1966), *Theory of self-reproducing automata,* ed. A. W. Burks, Urbana.

Webster, F. (1980), *The Guardian-Futures,* Jan 31st.

Weir, M. (1976), *Job satisfaction,* Fontana.

deWild, A. (1975), *Some social criteria for appropriate technology,* See McRobie (1975).

Wilkes, M. V. (1977), Babbage as a computer pioneer, *Historia Mathematica.* Vol 14.

Williams, T. J. (1978), Two decades of change – a review of the twenty year history of digital control, *Information technology,* ed. J. Moneta.

Winsbury, R. (1980), *The Guardian-Futures,* April 24th.

Youndon, E. (1979), *Learning to program in structural Cobol,* Prentice-Hall.

Zuse, K. (1962), *The outline of a computer development from mechanics to electronics,* See Randall (1973).

REPORTS

ACARD (1979), *Technological change: threats and opportunities for the United Kingdom.*

ACM (1968), Curriculum committee on computer science, Curriculum 68. *Recommendations for academic programs in computer science,* Communications ACM Vol 11.

ACM (1978), *History of programming languages conference,* Sigplan Notices Vol 13.

AOP (1979), *The ophthalmic optician* for AOP.

BIFU (1980), *Report of the BIFU microelectronics committee,* The Banking, Insurance and Finance Union.

CIS (1980), *Report on the new technology,* Counter information services.

COMSAT (1979), *Computer/satellite communications equipment phase 2, final report.*

CSE (1980), *Microelectronics: capitalist technology and the working class,* CSE Books.

DofE (1979), *The manpower implications of micro-electronic technology,* Department of Employment, HMSO.

NCAT (1978), *An alternative energy strategy for the United Kingdom,* National Centre for Alternative Technology.

NCCL (1968), *Privacy under attack,* National Council for Civil Liberties.

NEDC (1980), Progress report of the working party on electronic components.

SCCSD (1979), *The use of computers in the government,* Steering committee of the civil service departments.

Further Reading

There are many books dealing with the wide range of topics covered in this text. The following is a *short* list of suggestions for further reading. All volumes are referred to by the author's name; the book title and publisher can be found in the reference section.

For the historical background to computers, I recommend Morrison (1961), Goldstine (1972), Randall (1978), Lavington (1980) and Phillips (1978). With contemporary machines, general descriptions of how they work and their capabilities are to be found in Meek (1977), Hunt (1979), Laver (1976) and Simmons (1979). While I have not read all the many texts available on programming languages, I can suggest for Pascal — Moore (1980), BASIC — Alcock (1977), FORTRAN — Rohl (1977) and COBOL — Younden (1979). A guide to good programming practice in any language is given in Meek (1980).

For the background to the subject of appropriate technologies, readers should refer to any of the following: Scumacher (1974), Illich (1973), McRobie (1975) or Dickson (1974). As for the wide area of the impact of information technology and automation upon employment levels, education, social organisation and privacy, several works go beyond the scope of this book. These include Jenkins (1979), Barron (1979), Weir (1976), Davis (1979), Achoff (1978), McLuhan (1964), Nora (1978), Land (1979), Ashman (1979) and Hoffman (1980).

To keep abreast of new development and alternative approaches in all types of technology I would advise the regular perusal of the magazines New Scientist, Undercurrents and Personal Computer World.

Index